THE
Fresh
PASTA
COOKBOOK

THE
Fresh
PASTA
COOKBOOK

INTERNATIONAL RECIPES
FOR ALL SEASONS

BRIDGET JONES

BM

A QUINTET BOOK

This edition published in Canada by:
The Book Merchants Inc.
90 Nolan Court, Unit 5
Markham, Ontario
L3R 4L9

ISBN 0-7858-0-6490

Reprinted in 1994, 1995, 1998

This book was designed and produced by
Quintet Publishing Limited
6 Blundell Street
London N7 9BH

Creative Director: Richard Dewing
Designer: Ian Hunt
Project Editor: Katie Preston
Editor: Diana Vowles
Illustrator: Annie Ellis
Photographer: Trevor Wood

Typeset in Great Britain by
Central Southern Typesetters, Eastbourne
Manufactured in Singapore by
Colour Trend (Pte) Limited
Printed in Hong Kong by
Sing Cheong Printing Co. Ltd.

Contents

CHAPTER ONE

PASTA PERFECT
Every Time

*There is no great mystery involved in making simple, Italian-style pasta dough.
All it takes is a touch of muscle power for the kneading and rolling – unless, of
course, you have a pasta machine which will make light work of pounding the
ingredients to a smooth, pliable dough. It really is worth making your own dough,
if only for filled pasta such as tortellini and ravioli; apart from the variety of
fillings which you can introduce, homemade filled pasta is infinitely superior to
the average (or even slightly better) bought alternatives. Remember that you can
make a large batch of shapes when the mood takes you, fill them and freeze them
for future use.*

*The majority of the recipes in the chapters which follow do not necessarily need
homemade pasta. Most large supermarkets offer a range of fresh pasta shapes which
usually includes spirals or twists which you cannot make at home, egg noodles,
spaghetti, lasagne, paglia e fieno and fettucine. Flavored pasta doughs vary in
quality – spinach dough (verdi) is popular and tastes good but some of the herb-
flavored doughs taste inferior and, frankly, may ruin a good homemade sauce!
However, look out for Italian delicatessens offering good-quality
flavored pasta and fresh gnocchi.*
*Oriental noodles and pasta dough are also available fresh from specialist
supermarkets. Fresh Chinese egg noodles, won ton wrappers and rice sticks have
a finer flavor than the dried types and they also freeze extremely well, so it is worth
seeking out a source and buying a large batch. I include a recipe for won ton dough
which is not difficult to make and is a versatile wrapper for many types of dim sum
(snacks); however, flipping and flinging dough to form the long strands of fine egg noodles
is definitely a specialist technique.*
*The making of pasta can be immensely satisfying in itself, quite apart from the
dividends it pays in the quality of the final dish – so don a large apron, scrub
down the work surface and discover just how relaxing a pasta-making session can be.*

6

EQUIPMENT

You do not need any special equipment for making pasta. A large area of work surface helps, but it is not essential as you can always roll the dough in two or more batches. A mixing bowl, spoon and rolling pin are the basics, and an extra-long rolling pin is useful (make sure an ordinary one does not have knobs at the ends as they indent the dough and make rolling out difficult). You may also wish to invest in some of the following:

Pastry Wheel A fluted pastry wheel for cutting out ravioli.

Ravioli Pan A small metal pan with round or square hollows. Lay a sheet of pasta over the pan, press it in neatly and spoon mixture into the hollows. Brush with egg, cover with a second sheet of dough and roll the top to seal before cutting out the ravioli.

Pasta Machine A small but heavy metal machine for rolling pasta. Fitted with plain rollers which can be set at different distances apart, this basic, inexpensive machine is terrific. Once the dough is briefly kneaded, rolling it through the machine several times on the widest setting will complete the kneading.

Set the rollers at the narrow width for rolling out sheets of dough or substitute cutting rollers to make noodles or spaghetti. A ravioli filler attachment makes very small, neat ravioli by feeding the pasta and filling through a hopper-like attachment.

Electric Pasta Machines Large, expensive machines are available for mixing, kneading, rolling and extruding pasta. Unless you are an avid pasta eater, such a machine is an unlikely piece of equipment for the average domestic kitchen.

Pasta Dryer A small wooden rack on which to hang cut noodles or sheets of pasta as they are rolled out.

BELOW
Hand-turned pasta machine with attachments for filled pasta.

Dough Making

1 *Kneading pasta dough.*

2 *Rolling out pasta dough.*

3 *Pasta shapes made with cookie cutters.*

PASTA-MAKING TECHNIQUES

Mixing and Kneading

Unlike pastry, pasta dough needs a firm hand and a positive approach to mixing and kneading. The dough will seem very dry and prone to crumbling at first but as you knead it, the oil and egg combine fully with the flour and the ingredients bind together.

1 Mix the ingredients in the bowl, using a spoon at first, then your hand.

2 Begin the kneading process in the bowl, bringing the dough together and "wiping" the bowl clean of any crumbs.

3 Place the dough on a lightly floured, clean surface and knead it into a ball. Add a little flour to the work surface to prevent the dough sticking, but try to keep this to the minimum during kneading.

4 Once the dough has come together, knead it firmly and rhythmically, pressing it down and out in one movement, then pulling the edge of the dough back in toward the middle in the next movement. Keep turning the dough as you knead it, so that you work it around in a circle rather than constantly pressing and pulling one side. Keep the dough moving and it will not stick to the surface.

5 The dough is ready when it is smooth and warm. Wrap it in a plastic bag or plastic wrap and set it aside for 15–30 minutes if possible before rolling it out.

Rolling Out

When rolling the dough, try to keep it in the shape you want to end up with. Press the dough flat, forming it into an oblong or square, then roll it out firmly. Lift and "shake out" the dough a few times initially to insure it does not stick to the surface. As the dough becomes thinner you have to handle it more carefully to avoid splitting it. However, pasta dough is far more durable than pastry and the smoother it becomes as it is rolled, the tougher it is. It can be rolled out very thinly – until you can almost see through it – without breaking, but this is not essential for the majority of pasta dishes. Dust the surface under the dough with a little flour occasionally, as necessary, and dust the top, rubbing the flour over the dough with one hand. Continue rolling until the dough is thin and even – a common mistake is to leave the dough too thick, so that it becomes unpleasantly solid when cooked. For noodles, or pasta which is to be eaten plain or topped with sauce, try to roll out to the thickness of a piece of brown wrapping paper: this makes excellent noodles.

Make sure the surface under the dough is sifted with flour, then cover the dough completely with plastic wrap and leave for 10 minutes. This relaxes the dough before cutting – it is not essential but does prevent the dough from shrinking as it is cut.

ABOVE
Fruit and vegetable stall in Pienza, Italy.

Cutting Pasta

You need a large, sharp knife and a large floured platter or tray on which to place the pasta (a clean roasting pan will do). Flour the dough lightly before cutting. Once cut, keep the pasta dusted with flour to prevent it sticking together. Pasta may be dried before cooking by hanging it on a rack or spreading it out. I have, before now, draped pasta between two chair backs (covering them with paper towels first). Quite honestly, I have not found any great advantage to drying the pasta and have always felt that it is thoroughly inconvenient and unhygienic. It seems to cook well if it is added to boiling water straight after rolling.

Sheets Trim the dough edges so that they are straight, then cut the pasta into squares or oblongs. This is basic lasagne, so cut the dough to suit the size of dish.

Noodles Dust the dough well with flour, then roll it up. Use a sharp knife to cut the roll into ¼-inch wide slices. Shake out the slices as they are cut and they fall into long noodles. Keep the noodles floured and loosely piled on the tray to prevent them from sticking together. Cover loosely with plastic wrap.

Circles or shapes Use cookie cutters and aspic cutters to stamp out circles and shapes.

Squares Trim the dough edges, then use a clean, long ruler to cut the dough into wide strips. Cut these across into squares.

Small squares Use a ruler to cut the dough into 1-inch wide strips, then cut these across into squares. The small squares may be cooked and treated as bought pasta shapes.

Other shapes If you have the time, you can make other shapes by hand. Cut the dough into strips, then into small oblongs or squares. By twisting, pleating or pinching you can make bows and funny little twists and, I am sure, lots of clever alternatives. Frankly, I feel inclined to leave this to the manufacturers as it is very time-consuming.

LEFT
Homemade fresh pasta squares.

RIGHT
Homemade fresh pasta bows.

Cooking Fresh Pasta

Pasta should be cooked in enormous quantities of boiling water. Although you can get away with less water than the volume which is always suggested for authentic recipes (which means using a stock pot or catering-size kettle when cooking enough for four people), you need a large saucepan which holds 4–4½ quarts to cook ¾–1 pound of pasta. If you have a stock pot or very large pressure cooker which you can use without the lid on, so much the better.

Pour water into the pan to three-quarters of its capacity. Add salt and bring the water to a boil. Adding a little oil to the water helps to prevent it from frothing on the surface and boiling over rapidly – the pasta will not stick together if you have a pan which is large enough, and adding oil does little to prevent the pasta sticking in a pan which is too small! Add the pasta when the water is fully boiling, give it a stir and bring the water back to a boil rapidly. Be ready to reduce the heat, otherwise the water will froth over. Cook for about 3 minutes for noodles and other types of unfilled pasta. Filled pasta requires longer to allow the filling to cook through.

When cooked, the pasta should be "al dente" (with bite). It should be firm yet tender, not soft or sticky. Drain the cooked pasta at once, pouring it into a large strainer. Shake the strainer over the sink, then tip the pasta into a hot bowl and add the dressing or sauce. Serve at once.

Chilling Prepared Pasta

Dust the pasta with plenty of flour and place it in a large airtight container in the refrigerator. Cook within 2 days of making or freeze promptly. The unrolled dough may be wrapped and chilled for 1–2 days.

Leftover Cooked Pasta

Cool quickly and chill in a covered container. Reheat pasta in the microwave or in a sauce on the hob or in the oven.

Freezing Pasta

Uncooked fresh pasta freezes very well but it is best to roll and cut the dough first. Separate sheets of pasta by interleaving freezer film between them. Flour noodles and pack them loosely in plastic bags, then spread them out fairly flat for freezing, so they do not form a lump. Bought fresh pasta is an excellent freezer candidate which is ideal for impromptu meals.

Do not thaw frozen pasta before cooking, simply add it to boiling water and cook as for fresh pasta. Noodles and most other shapes take about the same time to cook as unfrozen pasta, once the water has come to a boil again. Frozen filled pasta requires extra cooking time to allow the filling to thaw and cook properly.

Cooked lasagne and cannelloni or similar layered pasta dishes freeze well but cooked shapes and noodles tend to have an inferior texture if frozen after cooking.

USING THE RECIPES

☛ Oven temperatures refer to conventional ovens; if you have a forced convection oven, please refer to the manufacturer's instructions for adapting cooking times or temperatures.

☛ Unless otherwise stated, herbs are fresh, not dried.

☛ Eggs are medium-size unless otherwise stated.

RIGHT
Traditional Italian ham and wines at a restaurant in Monte Reggiano, Tuscany.

RIGHT
Fresh pasta noodles ready for freezing.

PASTA PERFECT EVERY TIME

Pasta Dough

MAKES ABOUT 1 ¼ POUNDS PASTA

12 ounces hard flour
1 teaspoon salt
3 eggs
4 tablespoons olive oil
1 tablespoon water

Mix the flour and salt together in a large bowl. Make a well in the middle, then add the eggs, olive oil and water. Use a spoon to mix the eggs, oil and water, gradually working in the flour. When the mixture begins to bind into clumps, scrape the spoon clean and knead the dough together with your hands.

Press the dough into a ball and roll it around the bowl to leave the bowl completely clean of the mixture. Then place the dough on a lightly floured, clean surface and knead it thoroughly until it is smooth. Follow the notes on kneading (see page 9), keeping the dough moving and adding the minimum extra flour required to prevent it sticking as you work. Wrap the dough in a plastic bag and leave it to rest for 15–30 minutes before rolling it out. Do not chill the dough as this will make it difficult to handle.

Mixing the dough.

Flavored Pasta

The following may be used with the above recipe.

Beetroot Purée 2 ounces cooked and peeled beet with 2 eggs in a food processor or blender, or press it through a strainer (this eliminates dark speckles). Add the beet purée with the remaining egg. Omit the oil and water. Do not use beet which has been preserved in acetic acid or vinegar: it must be freshly boiled or the un-treated vacuum-packed type.

Carrot Omit half the oil and water but add 2 tablespoons carrot juice with the eggs. Pure carrot juice is available from natural foods stores and delicatessens.

Herb Add 4 tablespoons chopped mixed fresh herbs to the flour and salt. Suitable herbs include parsley, thyme, sage, tarragon, chives, chervil, marjoram and fennel. Rosemary may be used but only in very small quantities as it is a strongly flavored herb. Balance the delicate herbs against the stronger ones by using less of the latter. Use two, three or more herbs but remember that a delicate herb like dill will be totally lost if combined with many other herbs. Dill is best mixed with chives and a little parsley.

Olive Finely chop 4 ounces black olives and add them to the flour.

Spinach Wash and trim 8 ounces fresh spinach. Place the damp leaves in a saucepan. Cover tightly and cook over high heat for 5 minutes, shaking the pan often. Place the spinach in a strainer placed over a bowl. Press and squeeze all the juice from the spinach, leaving the leaves as dry as possible. Add 6 tablespoons spinach juice to the pasta and omit the oil and water.

Tomato Add 1 tablespoon concentrated tomato paste, beating it into the eggs.

Turmeric Add 1 teaspoon ground turmeric to the flour. For a pleasing, unusual, lightly spiced pasta, add 1 tablespoon white cumin seeds to the flour with the turmeric.

Walnut Use walnut oil instead of olive oil.

Won Ton Dough

MAKES ABOUT 12 OUNCES DOUGH

1½ cups all-purpose flour
½ cup cornstarch
pinch of salt
1 egg, beaten
½ cup water

Sift the flour, cornstarch and salt into a bowl, then make a well in the middle. Add the egg and pour in the water. Use a spoon to mix the egg and water into the flour. When the mixture binds together, scrape the spoon clean and use your hand to work the dough into a smooth ball, leaving the bowl free of mixture.

Place the dough on a clean surface and knead it thoroughly until it is very smooth. Cut the dough in half and wrap both portions in plastic wrap, then set aside for 15–30 minutes.

Roll out one portion of dough at a time. Dust the work surface and rolling pin lightly with cornstarch, then roll out the dough as required until it is thin and even.

When rolling out the dough for won tons, try to keep it in a square shape, then trim the edges. Use a clean, long ruler as a guide for cutting the dough in wide strips, then cut in the opposite direction to make squares.

Alternatively, a plain round cookie cutter may be used to stamp rounds out of the dough for making various dim sum, such as dumplings and packages.

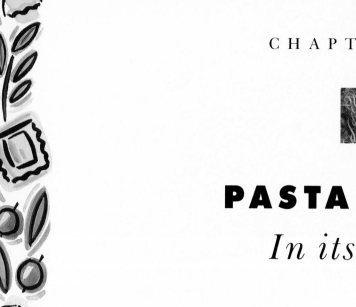

CHAPTER TWO

PASTA SIMPLE
In its Prime

The difference between fresh and dried pasta is most noticeable when it plays a prime role in a dish, with the minimum of additional ingredients. The recipes in this chapter highlight the ease of serving a simple pasta meal that delights the palate — the right mix of herbs or spices, a little fruit here and the tang of cheese there, or favorite everyday ingredients combined with satisfying success. Many of these dishes are quick to make and especially easy to serve. A few

large, colorful bowls are by far the best dishes in which to serve pasta, particularly these "throw-it-all-in" recipes. If you want to offer accompaniments, remember that old favorites are often the best: a good green salad and some warmed crusty bread are quite sufficient and often superfluous anyway, except for very hungry horses!

Pasta with Oil and Garlic

Good-quality olive oil and plump fresh garlic turn a plate of fresh pasta into a positive feast of a snack! You can increase the quantities of oil and garlic to suit your taste and serve with freshly grated parmesan if you like.

SERVES 4

½–⅔ cup olive oil
4 garlic cloves, chopped
freshly ground black pepper
1 pound tagliatelle or spaghetti

Heat the oil and garlic in a small saucepan. Cook the garlic very gently for 2 minutes – it should not fry rapidly, simply give up its flavor to the oil. Toss the oil and garlic and freshly ground black pepper into the drained pasta. Serve at once.

Pasta with Butter and Parmesan

SERVES 4

¾ stick (6 tablespoons) butter

¾ cup freshly grated Parmesan cheese

1 pound pasta

freshly ground black pepper

Whip the butter, then gradually mix in the Parmesan cheese and beat the mixture until it is soft and creamy. Dot it over the drained pasta, then toss well and add freshly ground black pepper to taste. Serve at once.

Spaghetti with Walnuts and Olives

SERVES 4

6 tablespoons olive oil

knob of butter

1 garlic clove, crushed (optional)

1½ cups finely chopped walnuts

¾ cup roughly chopped black olives

2 tablespoons capers, chopped

4 tablespoons chopped parsley

salt and freshly ground black pepper

1 pound spaghetti

Heat the oil and butter with the garlic (if using) until the butter melts. Stir in the walnuts, cook gently for 2 minutes, then add the olives, capers, parsley, a little salt and plenty of freshly ground black pepper. Pour the mixture over the drained spaghetti, toss well and serve at once.

BELOW
The beautiful area called Crete, south of Siena, Italy.

RIGHT
Spaghetti with Walnuts and Olives.

Tagliatelle with Chick Peas and Basil

Pasta and chick peas are two of my favorite savory foods – with aromatic fresh basil, this is a wonderful combination.

SERVES 4

4 tablespoons olive oil

1 garlic clove, crushed

6 tablespoons snipped chives

4 sage leaves, chopped

salt and freshly ground black pepper

2 × 14-ounce cans chick peas, drained

1 pound tagliatelle verdi

6 basil sprigs

Heat the olive oil, garlic, chives, sage, salt and freshly ground black pepper with the chick peas in a large saucepan for about 3 minutes. The idea is to heat the ingredients rather than to cook them. Add the drained pasta and toss well. Leave the pan over the lowest heat setting while you use scissors to shred the basil sprigs over the pasta, discarding any tough stalk ends. Mix lightly and serve.

Spirals with Grapes and Goat's Cheese

This is delicious for a light lunch or as a starter. Serve with slices of French bread.

SERVES 4

2 slices round goat cheese, each cut in 8 small wedges

6 ounces seedless green grapes

2 bunches of watercress, trimmed and roughly shredded

4 scallions, chopped

grated peel and juice of 1 orange

4 tablespoons olive oil

salt and freshly ground black pepper

12 ounces pasta spirals

Mix the cheese, grapes, watercress and scallions in a large bowl. Pour in the orange peel and juice and olive oil, then add a little salt and plenty of freshly ground black pepper. Mix well. Divide the hot, freshly drained pasta between four serving plates, then top each with a quarter of the cheese mixture. Serve at once.

Sun-dried Tomato and Vermouth Special

You can keep a jar of the dressing in the refrigerator for a couple of weeks for emergency pasta snacks!

SERVES 4

12 sun-dried tomatoes

¾ cup dry white vermouth

1 bay leaf

1 large marjoram sprig

½ cup olive oil

1 pound small pasta squares (page 14), spirals or broken spaghetti

freshly ground black pepper

1 red or white onion, very thinly sliced and separated into rings

freshly grated Parmesan cheese, to serve

Use a pair of kitchen scissors to snip the tomatoes into strips, then across into small pieces. Do this over a large screw-top jar. Add the vermouth, bay leaf and marjoram, then pour in the oil and cover the jar. Shake well and leave to stand for at least 3 hours – the longer the better, ideally overnight.

Tip the tomato mixture into a small saucepan and heat fairly slowly until just boiling. Reduce the heat so that the mixture barely bubbles and leave while you cook the pasta. Stir the tomatoes occasionally, then stir well just before pouring over the piping hot, drained pasta. Add the freshly ground black pepper and toss the pasta to coat all the pieces with the dressing. Top with the onion rings and serve with Parmesan cheese.

COOK'S TIP

Dried marjoram is too harsh for the sauce. If you do not have any fresh marjoram, add a very small sprig of thyme or a sage sprig instead. Onions with red or white skins have a mild flavor which makes them ideal for eating raw. I like the contrast between the crisp, zingy onion and the rather sultry dried tomato dressing.

Pasta with Ham and Two Peppers

SERVES 4

2 tablespoons dried red peppercorns, coarsely crushed

2 tablespoons dried green peppercorns, coarsely crushed

4 tablespoons chopped parsley

4 tablespoons snipped chives

½ cucumber, peeled

2 teaspoons chopped mint (optional)

1 pound pasta

½ stick (¼ cup) butter

12 ounces lean cooked ham, finely shredded

Mix the red and green peppercorns, parsley and chives. Cut the cucumber into 1-inch lengths, then slice these piece vertically and cut the slices into fine strips. Mix the mint into the cucumber strips.

While the pasta is cooking, melt the butter. Toss the hot butter and the ham into the drained pasta. Sprinkle the peppercorn mixture over and toss lightly. Top each portion with shredded cucumber and serve at once.

LEFT

Sun-dried Tomato and Vermouth Special.

Asparagus Supreme

This is really simple and quite unbeatable, especially if you are able to raid a pick-your-own farm for the freshest possible asparagus and cook the vegetable while it still spits with zest as you snap the stalks. If you are having a health-conscious spell, toss the asparagus in 1 tablespoon hot olive oil and mix some fromage frais into the pasta instead of using lots and lots of butter!

SERVES 4

1 pound asparagus, trimmed of woody ends if necessary
¾ stick (6 tablespoons) butter
salt and freshly ground black pepper
1 pound tagliatelle verdi or spinach-flavored small pasta squares (page 14)
3 tablespoons chopped fresh dill
freshly grated Parmesan cheese, to serve (optional)

Cook the asparagus in boiling salted water for 10–20 minutes, until just tender. If you do not have a tall asparagus saucepan, use the deepest pan you have and put the asparagus in it so that the tips stand above the rim. Tent foil over the top of the pan, crumpling it securely around the rim to seal in the steam. Very fresh, young asparagus will cook in 10 minutes, larger or more mature stalks take longer.

Heat the butter while the pasta is cooking. Drain the asparagus and cut the stalks into short lengths, then add them to the butter. Add a little seasoning, then pour the asparagus mixture over the drained pasta. Sprinkle with dill and mix well. Serve at once, with freshly grated Parmesan if you like.

Spaghetti with Smoked Sausage and Carrots

A good, inexpensive and satisfying supper dish: the sweetness of the carrot complements the flavorsome sausage. Try to find smoked sausage made with fresh garlic.

SERVES 4

3 tbsp olive oil
1 onion, halved and thinly sliced
8 oz carrots, coarsely grated
1 lb smoked sausage, cut into strips
salt and freshly ground black pepper
1 lb spaghetti
2 oz butter

Heat the oil in a large frying pan. Add the onion and cook for 5 minutes, then add the carrots and sausage. Cook, stirring often, for about 10 minutes, until the pieces of sausage are browned in parts and the carrots are lightly cooked. Add seasoning to taste. Add the butter to the carrot and sausage mixture, toss the lot into the drained spaghetti and serve at once.

Fresh Green Pasta

This combination of ingredients also makes an excellent salad. If you use very small pasta squares, the hot mixture may also be served in scooped-out tomatoes as a first course.

SERVES 4

8 ounces shelled or frozen peas
4 tablespoons olive oil or ½ stick (¼ cup) butter
4 scallions, chopped
2 avocados, halved and cut into chunks
juice of ½ lemon
salt and freshly ground black pepper
1 pound pasta verdi
1 tablespoon chopped mint
mint sprigs, to garnish (optional)

Cook the peas in boiling salted water for 10 minutes. Heat the oil or melt the butter in a saucepan. Add the scallions and cook for 1 minute, then stir in the peas, avocado and lemon juice. Season to taste.

Toss the pea and avocado mixture into the drained pasta. Sprinkle the mint over and serve at once. Mint sprigs may be added as a garnish if liked.

Egg and Tomato Favorite

Familiar foods that go together well make this slightly unusual yet reassuring homely dish.

SERVES 4

1 pound tomatoes, peeled and roughly chopped (see Cook's Tip)
salt and freshly ground black pepper
4 tablespoons chopped parsley
8 eggs
large knob of butter
1 pound pasta
freshly grated Parmesan or Cheddar cheese, to serve

Place the tomatoes in a bowl and season them well, then mix in the parsley. Place the eggs in a saucepan, cover with cold water and bring to a boil. Cook for 10 minutes, then drain. Shell the eggs under cold water so as not to burn your fingers and place them in a bowl, then cut them into eighths.

Toss the hot eggs and butter into the pasta, then mix in the tomatoes when the butter has melted. Serve at once, topping each portion with grated cheese.

COOK'S TIP

To peel tomatoes, place them in a bowl and pour boiling water over them. Leave to stand for 30–60 seconds: ripe tomatoes are ready quickly, under-ripe fruit may require an extra 30 seconds. Split the skins with a sharp, pointed knife and they will rub off easily.

Tagliatelle with Sesame Cabbage

Herb-flavored tagliatelle is ideal for this recipe.

SERVES 4

4 tablespoons sunflower oil
1 large onion, chopped
1 garlic clove, crushed
3 tablespoons sesame seeds
3 tablespoons currants
salt and freshly ground black pepper
1 pound red or white cabbage, shredded
1 tablespoon cider vinegar
1 pound tagliatelle

Heat the oil, then add the onion, garlic, sesame seeds and currants. Add seasoning to taste. Cook, stirring often, over moderate to low heat for about 20 minutes, until the onion is well cooked. Stir in the cabbage and cook for about 10 minutes, stirring often, so that the cabbage is lightly cooked and still crunchy. Add the cider vinegar and stir well.

Toss the cabbage mixture with the freshly drained tagliatelle and serve at once.

Smoked Tofu with Squares

Pasta flavored with herbs or tomatoes goes very well with smoked tofu. If you do not want to make your own pasta, buy fresh spirals or paglia e fieno.

SERVES 4

2 tablespoons olive oil
¼ stick (2 tablespoons) butter
4 celery stalks, finely diced
1 green bell pepper, seeded and diced
salt and freshly ground black pepper
1 pound smoked tofu (bean curd), cut into small cubes
grated peel of 1 lemon
2 scallions, finely chopped
3 tablespoons chopped parsley
1 pound small pasta squares (page 14)
lemon wedges, to serve

Heat the oil and butter in a large saucepan. Add the celery and cook, stirring, for 5 minutes. Add the green bell pepper, a little salt and plenty of freshly ground black pepper, stir well and cook gently for a further 10 minutes. Lightly mix the tofu into the bell pepper and celery mixture, then leave to heat through for about 5 minutes.

Mix the lemon peel, scallions and parsley. Toss the drained pasta with the tofu mixture and serve in individual bowls. Sprinkle with the lemon peel, scallion and parsley mixture and serve with lemon wedges. The juice from the lemon may be squeezed over the pasta.

BELOW
The Ponte Vecchio in Florence.

Pasta with Eggs and Tarragon

An easy dish that makes a tasty change from poached eggs on toast! Serve half portions for a starter or light snack.

SERVES 4

¾ stick (6 tablespoons) butter (or use olive oil or a mixture of butter and olive oil if preferred)
3 tablespoons chopped tarragon
8 eggs
1 pound pasta (tagliatelle, paglia e fieno or spirals)
freshly ground black pepper
freshly grated Parmesan cheese, to serve

Warm four plates or bowls. Melt the butter (or heat the oil with the butter if used) and add the tarragon, then set aside over very low heat. Poach the eggs when the pasta is just ready for draining.

Divide the pasta between the plates or bowls. Place a couple of eggs on each portion, then spoon the butter and tarragon over the top. Season with black pepper and serve at once with grated Parmesan cheese.

Pasta with Mixed Mushrooms

SERVES 4

½ cup dried mushrooms

1¼ cups dry white wine

½ stick (¼ cup) butter

8 ounces crimini mushrooms, sliced

8 ounces oyster mushrooms, sliced

1¼ cups light cream

salt and freshly ground black pepper

3 tablespoons chopped parsley

1 pound pasta

freshly grated Parmesan cheese, to serve

Place the dried mushrooms in a bowl and pour the wine over them. Cover with a saucer and weight it down to keep the mushrooms submerged in the wine. Leave for 30 minutes. Discard any tough stalks and slice the mushrooms if necessary (they are usually sold sliced in packets).

Melt the butter in a large saucepan. Add the crimini mushrooms and cook for 5 minutes, stirring, then pour in the dried mushrooms and wine from soaking. Bring to a boil, reduce the heat and cook at a steady simmer for 15 minutes. Stir in the oyster mushrooms, cook for 2–3 minutes, then add the cream, seasoning and parsley. Heat gently, stirring, but do not boil or the sauce will curdle.

Add the drained pasta to the sauce, remove from the heat and mix well. Allow to stand, covered, for 2–3 minutes, then toss the pasta again and serve with grated Parmesan cheese.

Pasta Carbonara

SERVES 4

½ stick (¼ cup) butter

12 ounces cooked ham, shredded

8 eggs

salt and freshly ground black pepper

⅔ cup light cream

1 pound tagliatelle

plenty of chopped parsley

freshly grated Parmesan cheese, to serve

BELOW
*Looking across the Tuscan hills
from San Gimignano.*

Melt the butter in a large, heavy-bottomed or non-stick saucepan. Add the ham and cook for 2 minutes. Beat the eggs with seasoning and the cream. Reduce the heat under the pan, if necessary, then pour in the eggs and cook them gently, stirring all the time until they are creamy. Do not cook the eggs until they set and scramble and do not increase the heat to speed up the process or the carbonara will be spoiled.

The pasta should be added to the boiling water at the same time as adding the eggs to the pan. This way, the pasta will be drained and hot, ready to be tipped into the eggs. When the eggs are half set, add the pasta, mix well until the eggs are creamy and serve at once, sprinkled with parsley. Offer Parmesan cheese with the pasta carbonara.

CHAPTER THREE

DRESSINGS AND SAUCES
For Fresh Pasta

It is very difficult to select a group of sauces for such an essential chapter because there are so many possibilities that the list can become endless. I have included the basic recipes which are often used in composite pasta dishes – a meat ragout, a tomato sauce and a selection of milk-based sauces; there are also other familiar sauce recipes which make versatile standbys. However, in addition, you will find a good selection of different sauces to surprise the taste buds.

Remember that many sauces freeze well, so it can be worth having a batch-cooking session, both for making fresh pasta and for preparing the sauces. Tomato sauce, in particular, is really worth making in quantity when tomatoes are either inexpensive or good flavor-wise.

Look out for plum tomatoes, as they make excellent sauces. There are suggestions about the choice of pasta in some recipes; apart from the practicalities of what you feel like making or the range of fresh pasta in your local supermarket, think about the shape of the pasta and the texture of the sauce when you are looking for the perfect match.

Big, chunky sauces can be difficult to eat with long, fine pasta such as spaghetti, and very small pasta shapes can be lost with either a thin sauce or a chunky one. This may seem to be a minor point, yet it is strange how shape and size can alter the balance of the dish and impair the enjoyment of it. In the absence of a vast variety, good old ribbon noodles, tagliatelle or fettucine as they may be called, taste good with most sauces!

Cardamom Fish Sauce

Lemon and cilantro pep up plain white fish in this delicious sauce. It is particularly good with spirals or small pieces of pasta, such as squares or cut-up spaghetti; saffron or turmeric pasta is ideal if you are making your own. For a first course, serve half quantities of sauce in small rings of saffron or turmeric noodles.

SERVES 4

¼ stick (2 tablespoons) butter

1 small onion, finely chopped

1 red bell pepper, seeded and diced

6 green cardamoms

1 bay leaf

grated peel of 1 lemon

¼ cup all-purpose flour

1¼ cups fish stock

salt and freshly ground black pepper

1½ pounds white fish fillet, skinned and cut into chunks

1¼ cups light cream

2 tablespoons chopped cilantro leaves

Melt the butter in a saucepan. Add the onion, bell pepper, cardamoms, bay leaf and lemon peel. Press the cardamoms to split them slightly, then cook gently for 20 minutes, until the onion and bell pepper are well cooked. Stir often, so that the bay and spices give up their flavor and the onions do not brown.

Stir in the flour, then gradually pour in the stock, stirring all the time, and bring to a boil. Reduce the heat, if necessary, so that the sauce just simmers – it will be too thick at this stage. Add seasoning and the fish. Stir lightly, then cover the pan and cook gently for 20 minutes, or until the fish is cooked. Gently stir in the cream, then heat through without boiling. Taste for seasoning before serving sprinkled with the cilantro.

35

Salmon with Dill and Mustard

Although delicate, salmon is a rich fish and the piquancy of this mustard sauce complements it perfectly. For classic simplicity, arrange the fish and its dressing on homemade egg noodles; or add a zesty note to the pasta by mixing the grated peel of 1 lemon with the flour when mixing the dough. The dill must be fresh – forget the recipe when you only have dried dillweed as it will make the sauce taste as though you have used grass cuttings.

SERVES 4

1½–2 pounds salmon fillet, skinned

salt and freshly ground black pepper

4 tablespoons olive oil

1 tablespoon lemon juice

½ onion, finely chopped

2 tablespoons all-purpose flour

⅔ cup milk

4 tablespoons Dijon or other mild mustard

1¼ cups soured cream

3 tablespoons chopped dill

¼ cucumber, peeled and finely diced

1 celery stalk, finely diced

Lay the salmon on a large piece of double-thick foil. Season it really well, then sprinkle with 1 tablespoon of the oil and the lemon juice. Broil the fish for about 15 minutes, or until cooked through.

Meanwhile, heat the remaining oil in a saucepan and add the onion. Cook, stirring, for 10 minutes. Stir in the flour and cook for 3 minutes before stirring in the milk, then bring to a boil. Beat the mustard into the thick sauce, then stir in the cream and heat gently but do not boil. Finally, stir in the dill and remove from the heat, then taste for seasoning.

Mix the cucumber and celery. Drain the cooking liquid from the salmon into the sauce. Use two forks to separate the cooked salmon into large chunks. Mix the mustard and dill sauce into the pasta, then lightly mix in the fish. Divide between serving platters and top each portion with a little of the cucumber and celery.

COOK'S TIP

Fresh dill freezes well for use in sauces but it will not retain its shape for garnishing. The herb thaws quickly and becomes limp; however, it crushes easily in its packet while frozen, separating the stalks from the fine fronds. If crushed and measured while frozen, the dill will not need chopping.

Anchovy and Egg Cream Sauce

This sauce is quick to prepare for unexpected guests, especially if you keep some cream in the freezer. Good with spaghetti, noodles or shapes and ideal, in small quantities, for a first course.

SERVES 4

8 eggs
1 2-ounce can anchovy fillets
4 scallions, chopped
1¼ cups light cream
freshly ground black pepper
plenty of shredded basil or chopped parsley

Place the eggs in a saucepan and cover with cold water. Bring to a boil, then cook for 8 minutes. Meanwhile, drain the oil from the anchovies into a small pan. Add the scallions and cook for 2 minutes. Chop the anchovy fillets, add them to the scallions, then stir in the cream and add pepper to taste. Heat very gently but do not allow to simmer or the cream will curdle.

Shell and roughly chop the eggs, then mix them into the sauce with basil or parsley. Serve at once, tossed into the hot pasta.

Tonnato Dressing

Tonnato is a cold sauce which is traditionally served with cold cooked veal; however, this versatile tuna mayonnaise is excellent on freshly cooked pasta of any type – try making olive-flavored noodles and serve them as a first course topped with this sauce. The sauce is also good tossed with cold cooked pasta and served on a green salad base to make a tempting cocktail.

SERVES 4

2 egg yolks
juice of 1 lemon
salt and freshly ground black pepper
1 7-ounce can tuna in oil
scant 1 cup olive oil
⅔ cup sour cream, fromage frais or Greek-style yogurt (optional)
2 tablespoons capers, chopped
chopped parsley, to serve

Place the egg yolks in a bowl. Use an electric beater to whisk in the lemon juice and a little seasoning. Whisk in the oil drained from the can of tuna. Whisking all the time on high speed, trickle in the olive oil very slowly. If you add the oil too quickly, the mixture will curdle; however, once it begins to thicken into a creamy mayonnaise, the oil can be poured in more quickly.

Mash the tuna fish to a paste, then mix it into the mayonnaise. Stir in the cream, fromage frais or yogurt (if used) and the capers. (The cream, fromage frais or yogurt lighten the sauce slightly.) Taste for seasoning before serving and sprinkle the pasta and sauce with chopped parsley.

COOK'S TIP

Cheating is invited here! Use 1¼ cups good-quality mayonnaise (not the cheaper, acidic type) instead of making your own. Alternatively, for a low-fat version, mash the tuna and stir in a mixture of low-fat soft cheese and fromage frais.

Piquant Shrimp and Tomato Sauce

Good with spaghetti or noodles, this sauce may also be layered with lasagne, then covered with a creamy topping and baked.

SERVES 4

| 2 tablespoons oil |
| 2 garlic cloves, crushed |
| 2 green chilies, seeded and chopped |
| 1 large onion, chopped |
| 1 green bell pepper, seeded and diced |
| 1 carrot, diced |
| 2 celery stalks, diced |
| 1 bay leaf |
| 2 × 14-ounce cans chopped tomatoes |
| 1 tablespoon tomato paste |
| 1 teaspoon sugar |
| salt and freshly ground black pepper |
| 1 pound frozen peeled cooked shrimp |
| 2 tablespoons chopped cilantro leaves |

Heat the oil in a large saucepan. Add the garlic, chilies, onion, green bell pepper, carrot, celery and bay leaf. Cook, stirring, for 20 minutes. Then stir in the tomatoes, tomato paste, sugar and plenty of seasoning. Bring to a boil, reduce the heat, cover and simmer gently for 30 minutes.

Add the shrimp, stir well and cook for 15 minutes, or until they are hot through. Taste for seasoning, then ladle the sauce over the pasta and top with the cilantro.

Seafood Medley

You can vary the mixture of seafood according to your budget, the choice at the fishmarket and personal preference. Remember to add delicate ingredients at the end so they do not overcook. Serve with plain pasta or try combining a mixture of tomato, spinach and plain pasta.

SERVES 4

| 1 quart mussels |
| 1 bay leaf |
| 1¼ cups dry white wine |
| 6 tablespoons olive oil |
| 1 onion, halved and thinly sliced |
| 1 celery stalk, finely diced |
| 1 green bell pepper, seeded and finely diced |
| 3 garlic cloves, crushed |
| grated peel of 1 lemon |
| salt and freshly ground black pepper |
| 4 small squid, cleaned and sliced |
| 12 ounces goosefish fillet, cut in small chunks |
| 6–8 scallops, shelled and sliced |
| 12 ounces peeled cooked shrimp, thawed if frozen |
| 8 black olives, pitted and chopped |
| plenty of chopped parsley |
| freshly grated Parmesan cheese, to serve |

Scrub the mussels and scrape off any barnacles or dirt on the shell. Pull away the black beard which protrudes from the shell. Discard any open mussels which do not shut when tapped. Place the mussels in a large pan and add the bay leaf and wine. Bring to a boil, then put a close-fitting lid on the pan and reduce the heat slightly so that the wine does not

Seafood Medley.

boil too rapidly. Cook for about 10 minutes, shaking the pan often, until all the mussels are open. Discard any that are shut. Strain the mussels, reserving the cooking liquor and bay leaf. Reserve a few mussels for garnish, if you like, and use a fork to remove the others from their shells.

Heat the oil in a large saucepan. Add the reserved bay leaf, onion, celery, green pepper, garlic, lemon rind and plenty of seasoning. Cover and cook, stirring occasionally, for 20 minutes, or until the onion is softened but not browned. Pour in the reserved cooking liquor, bring to a boil and boil hard for about 3 minutes, or until reduced by half. Then reduce the heat and add the squid. Cover the pan and simmer for 5 minutes. Add the goosefish, cover the pan again and cook for a further 5 minutes. Next, add the scallops and cook gently for 3 minutes, or until the seafood is just cooked.

Add the shrimp, mussels and olives. Heat gently, then taste for seasoning. Stir in plenty of parsley and serve at once, with Parmesan cheese to sprinkle over the seafood and pasta.

COOK'S TIP

To clean squid, first wash it. Pull the head and tentacles from the body sac. Cut the tentacles off just above the head and slice them if you want to add them to the dish. Discard the other head parts and innards. Pull out the transparent quill which is inside the body sac, then rinse the sac well. Rub off the spotted skin to leave the squid clean and white. The flaps may rub off and these can be sliced separately. Slice the sac in thin rings.

Chicken and Tarragon Sauce

This is a simple sauce which goes well with any pasta. It may also be layered with lasagne, noodles or shapes in baked dishes. Turkey may be used instead of chicken.

SERVES 4

¹/₄–¹/₂ stick (2–4 tablespoons) butter

1 small onion, finely chopped

1 bay leaf

4 ounces button mushrooms, sliced

¹/₃ cup all-purpose flour

1¹/₄ cups chicken stock

²/₃ cup milk

*8–12 ounces boneless, skinned,
cooked chicken, diced*

2 tablespoons chopped tarragon

salt and freshly ground black pepper

²/₃ cup light cream

Melt ¼ stick (2 tablespoons) of the butter in a saucepan. Add the onion and bay leaf and cook, stirring occasionally, for 15 minutes, or until the onion is softened slightly but not browned. Add the mushrooms and continue to cook for 10–15 minutes, until they give up their juice and this evaporates completely, leaving the reduced vegetables and the butter.

Stir in the flour, then gradually pour in the stock and bring to a boil, stirring all the time. Stir in the milk, bring back to a boil, then add the chicken and tarragon with seasoning to taste. Reduce the heat, cover the pan and simmer gently for 10 minutes. Stir in the cream and heat gently without boiling. If you like, beat in the remaining butter to enrich the sauce and make it rather special.

Duck and Orange Dressing

A rich dressing for narrow noodles or spaghetti, and a good way of making a couple of large duck breasts serve four. Make a salad of grated zucchini and carrot as an accompaniment (see Cook's Tip).

SERVES 4

2 large boneless duck breasts, skinned and cut into fine strips

1 tablespoon all-purpose flour

salt and freshly ground black pepper

½ teaspoon ground mace

grated peel and juice of 1 orange

1 tablespoon oil

1 onion, halved and thinly sliced

12 ounces button mushrooms, sliced

1¼ cups dry red wine

4 tablespoons redcurrant jelly

Place the duck meat in a bowl or plastic bag. Add the flour, plenty of seasoning, the mace and orange peel. Mix well, or close and shake the bag.

Heat the oil in a large skillet pan. Add the duck and brown the strips all over, then add the onion and cook, stirring often, for about 15 minutes, or until the onion is softened slightly but not browned. Stir in the mushrooms and cook for 10 minutes or so, until they are well reduced. Pour in the orange juice and wine, then bring to a boil. Add the redcurrant jelly and boil for about 1 minute, stirring.

Taste for seasoning, then ladle the duck sauce over the pasta and serve at once.

COOK'S TIP

Carrot and Zucchini Salad. Coarsely grate 3 carrots and 3 zucchini. Mix with a finely chopped scallion and 4 shredded basil sprigs. Add 2 tablespoons olive oil, a squeeze of orange juice and seasoning. Serve on a bed of iceberg lettuce.

Leek and Turkey Sauce

Boneless turkey breast fillets are versatile and inexpensive when combined with bulky vegetables and pasta. This is another sauce to serve with any pasta or to use in baked dishes and layer with lasagne.

SERVES 4

12 ounces boneless turkey breast fillet, skinned and diced
4 tablespoons all-purpose flour
salt and freshly ground black pepper
2 tablespoons oil
1 pound leeks, sliced
2 tablespoons chopped sage
1 1/4 cups dry cider
1 1/4 cups turkey or chicken stock
2 tablespoons freshly grated Parmesan cheese
2 ounces mozzarella cheese, chopped
2/3 cup Greek-style yogurt
a little paprika

Coat the turkey with the flour and plenty of seasoning. Heat the oil in a large saucepan. Add the turkey and cook, stirring often, until lightly browned. Add the leeks and sage, stir well, then cover the pan and cook for 15 minutes, stirring once or twice, until the leeks are greatly reduced in volume.

Stir in the cider and stock, then bring to a boil, stirring, and reduce the heat. Cover and simmer for 15 minutes, until the leeks are cooked. Stir in the Parmesan and mozzarella, and taste for seasoning. When the cheeses have melted, stir in the yogurt and remove the pan from the heat. Serve at once, poured over pasta or tossed with it. Dust with a little paprika.

BELOW
Brilliantly colored plants in the window of a house in Siena, Italy.

Chicken in Blue

Blue cheese makes a rich sauce for chicken or turkey. Serve large quantities of plain fresh pasta noodles to balance the full flavor of the sauce. I have used Danish blue but any other blue cheese may be substituted – dolcelatte, for example, or tangy gorgonzola for a really powerful flavor.

SERVES 4

2 tablespoons olive oil
1 garlic clove, crushed
1 red bell pepper, seeded and diced
1 pound boneless chicken, skinned and diced
salt and freshly ground black pepper
8 ounces small button mushrooms
4 tablespoons dry white wine
2/3 cup light cream
8 ounces Danish blue cheese, cut into small pieces
2 scallions, finely chopped
2 tablespoons chopped parsley

Heat the oil in a large skillet. Add the garlic, red bell pepper and chicken with some seasoning – go easy on the salt at this stage as the blue cheese can make the sauce quite salty. Cook, stirring often, for about 20 minutes, or until the diced chicken is lightly browned and cooked.

Add the mushrooms and cook for 2 minutes, then pour in the wine and bring to a boil. Turn the heat to the lowest setting and make sure the mixture has stopped boiling before pouring in the cream and stirring in the cheese. Stir over low heat until the cheese has melted. Do not allow the sauce to simmer or it will curdle.

When the cheese has melted, taste the sauce, then pour it over the pasta and sprinkle with the scallions and parsley. Serve at once.

Steak Sauce with Salsa

A really simple steak sauce, this one, with some onion and mushrooms to complement the flavor of the meat. The taste-bud awakener is the salsa – a Mexican-style cold sauce of tomato, onion and chili. Serve it in a separate dish so that it can be spooned over the beef and pasta to taste. Noodles or spaghetti are the ideal pasta for this.

SERVES 4

8 ounces ripe tomatoes, peeled (see Cook's Tip, page 26)	grated peel and juice of ½ lime
1 red onion, finely chopped	3 tablespoons chopped cilantro leaves
2 fresh green chilies, seeded and chopped	1½ pounds lean sirloin steak, sliced across the grain and cut into strips (see Cook's Tip)
1 garlic clove, crushed	3 tablespoons all-purpose flour
salt and freshly ground black pepper	large knob of beef drippings or 2 tablespoons oil
1 teaspoon superfine sugar	1 large onion, halved and thinly sliced
	1 bay leaf
	2 parsley sprigs
	2 thyme sprigs
	12 ounces button mushrooms, sliced
	good beef stock or canned consommé
	dash of Worcestershire sauce

Make the salsa first but not too far in advance of serving. Halve the tomatoes, discard the cores leading from the stalks, then chop them. Mix with the onion, chilies and garlic. Add plenty of seasoning, the sugar, lime peel and juice, and the cilantro. Mix well. Taste to check the seasoning and set aside.

Toss the steak with the flour and plenty of seasoning. Melt the drippings or heat the oil in a large skillet. When the fat is shimmering hot, add the steak and stir-fry the strips until they are browned. If the fat is hot enough, and particularly if using drippings, the strips will seal, brown and cook quickly. Add the onion and herbs, reduce the heat and cook for 15 minutes, or until the onion is softened slightly. Stir in the mushrooms and cook for a further 15 minutes.

Pour in the stock and add Worcestershire sauce to taste. Bring to a boil, stirring, reduce the heat and simmer gently for 5 minutes. Taste for seasoning and remove the herb sprigs before serving.

COOK'S TIP

When cutting steak for frying as above, slice the meat across the grain, then cut the slices into strips. If the meat is cut with the grain the result is not as tender.

Rich Meat Ragout

This is a good Bolognese-style sauce for ladling over pasta or layering with it.

SERVES 4

3 tablespoons olive oil
1 large onion, chopped
2 celery stalks, finely diced
2 carrots, finely diced
1 green bell pepper, seeded and diced
2 garlic cloves, crushed
4 ounces rindless smoked bacon, diced
2 teaspoons dried marjoram
1 thyme sprig
1 bay leaf
8 ounces lean ground pork
8 ounces lean ground braising steak
salt and freshly ground black pepper
1 tablespoon all-purpose flour
1 tablespoon tomato paste
2 × 14-ounce cans chopped tomatoes
1¼ cups dry red wine
4 tablespoons chopped parsley
freshly grated Parmesan cheese, to serve

Heat the oil in a large, heavy-based saucepan. Add the onion, celery, carrots, green bell pepper, garlic, bacon, marjoram, thyme and bay leaf. Cook, stirring, until the onion is slightly softened and the bacon cooked – about 15 minutes.

Add the pork and steak and continue to cook, stirring, for 10 minutes to mix and cook the meats lightly. Stir in plenty of seasoning, the flour and tomato paste. Stir in the tomatoes and wine, then bring the sauce to a boil. Reduce the heat, cover, and simmer the sauce for 1½ hours. Stir the sauce occasionally during cooking.

At the end of cooking, taste and adjust the seasoning before mixing in the parsley and serving the sauce ladled over pasta. Serve with Parmesan cheese.

Pork with Dates and Ginger

Serve this sweet and slightly spicy dish with plain fine noodles or tagliatelle and a fresh onion salad (see Cook's Tip).

SERVES 4

2 tablespoons oil

1/2 cup peeled, chopped fresh ginger root

1 cinnamon stick

1 1/2 pounds lean boneless pork, diced

salt and freshly ground black pepper

4 ounces fresh dates

2/3 cup fresh orange juice

2/3 cup water

2/3 cup sour cream

Heat the oil in a skillet. Add the ginger root, cinnamon and pork. Sprinkle in plenty of seasoning, then cook, stirring occasionally, until the pork is lightly browned and cooked through.

Meanwhile, slit the dates and remove their pits, then rub off their papery skins and slice the fruit. Add the orange juice and water to the pork. Bring to a boil, reduce the heat and simmer hard for 10 minutes. Stir in the dates, simmer for 5 minutes and taste for seasoning.

Remove the pan from the heat, swirl in the sour cream and serve at once, ladled over individual portions of pasta.

COOK'S TIP

Fresh Onion Salad. Thinly slice 2 red or white onions. Separate the slices into rings and place them in a bowl of iced water. Leave to soak for 30 minutes, or up to an hour. Drain well and pat dry on paper towels. Trim and roughly chop 1 bunch of watercress. Cut the tops from a tub of cress. Mix both types of cress and the onions. Sprinkle with salt, a little lemon juice and a little olive oil. Dust with paprika and serve.

Jalapeño Beef and Yam

Here's a recipe to transform old-fashioned stewed beef into a multi-national meal! Of course, a plain beef stew tastes really good with pasta but this is a bit different and the combination of yams and bell peppers makes the beef go a lot further.

SERVES 4

1 pound lean chuck steak, diced quite small
2 tablespoons all-purpose flour
salt and freshly ground black pepper
2 tablespoons oil or knob of beef drippings
2 onions, chopped
2½ cups water
1½ pounds yam, peeled and cut into 1-inch cubes
2 garlic cloves, crushed
1 red bell pepper, seeded and diced
1 green bell pepper, seeded and diced
1 4-ounce can jalapeño chilies, drained and chopped
1 ounce currants
grated peel and juice of 1 lime
2 tablespoons chopped cilantro leaves
2 teaspoons thyme leaves

Set the oven at 350°F. Coat the meat with flour and plenty of salt. Add a little pepper. Heat half the oil or drippings in a flameproof casserole. Add the meat and brown the pieces all over, then add half the chopped onion and cook for a few minutes. Pour in the water and bring to a boil. Cover the casserole tightly and transfer it to the oven. Cook for 1 hour, then reduce the heat to 325°F and cook for a further 2 hours, or until the meat is very tender. Stir occasionally, scraping the side of the casserole to remove any residue which bakes on above the line of the stew.

Meanwhile, cook the yam in boiling water for 10 minutes, or until just tender. Drain. Heat the remaining oil or drippings and add the rest of the onion with the garlic, red and green bell peppers, chilies and currants. Cook over medium heat, stirring often, for 20 minutes, until the onion and bell peppers are well cooked. Stir in the lime peel and juice and herbs. Add the yam and mix well. Remove from the heat, cover and set aside until the beef is cooked. It is a good idea to prepare the yam mixture immediately after the steak, so that the flavors have time to mingle and develop.

Stir the yam mixture into the stew and reheat thoroughly on the hob before serving. Ladle the sauce over bowls of tagliatelle or pasta shapes.

Sausage Meatball Sauce

SERVES 4

1 pound pork sausage meat

1 onion, finely chopped

1 garlic clove, crushed

¼ teaspoon chili powder

1 teaspoon ground coriander

salt and freshly ground black pepper

1 teaspoon dried oregano

1 teaspoon chopped thyme

1 tablespoon chopped sage

1½ cups fresh bread crumbs

1 egg

1 tablespoon oil

1 green bell pepper, seeded and diced

8 ounces button mushrooms

½ quantity Good Tomato Sauce (page 56)

Place the sausage meat in a bowl. Add the onion, garlic, chili, coriander, seasoning, oregano, thyme, sage and bread crumbs. Use a mixing spoon to break up the sausage meat and mix in some of the other ingredients. When the sausage meat is well broken up, add the egg. Then pound the ingredients together until thoroughly combined.

Wash your hands, then rinse them under cold water and keep them wet while you shape the meatballs to prevent the mixture sticking to them. Shape small, walnut-size meatballs.

Heat the oil in a large skillet. Add the meatballs and brown them all over, using a spoon and fork to roll them around the skillet. Add the green bell pepper and mushrooms and continue to cook for 10 minutes, or until the bell pepper is softened slightly. Pour in the tomato sauce and bring to a boil. Simmer for 20 minutes, turning the meatballs in the sauce occasionally. Serve piping hot.

Eggplant and Leek Topping

SERVES 4

2 large eggplants, trimmed and cubed

salt and freshly ground black pepper

about 4 tablespoons olive oil

2 garlic cloves, crushed

¼ teaspoon chili powder

1 pound leeks, sliced

2 tablespoons tahini

1¾ cups stock (vegetable or chicken)

Place the eggplants in a strainer and sprinkle them with salt, then leave them to stand over a bowl for 20 minutes. Rinse the eggplants well and leave to drain.

Heat half the olive oil in a large saucepan. Add some of the eggplant cubes and brown them on all sides. Use a slotted spoon to remove the cubes from the pan and set aside. Add more oil as necessary and cook the remaining cubes. Set aside. Add the garlic, chili powder and leeks to the pan, then cook, stirring often, for 10 minutes, until the leeks are greatly reduced in volume.

Replace the eggplant cubes and stir in the tahini, then pour in the stock and bring to a boil. Reduce the heat and cover the pan, then simmer for 15–20 minutes, until the eggplants and leeks are cooked through. Taste for seasoning before serving.

Broccoli and Baby Corn Dressing

SERVES 4

1 pound broccoli, cut into small flowerets

8 ounces whole baby corn cobs

¼ stick (2 tablespoons) butter or 2 tablespoons oil

1 onion, chopped

8 ounces rindless bacon, diced

1 tablespoon all-purpose flour

salt and freshly ground black pepper

6 tablespoons dry sherry

⅔ cup chicken or vegetable stock

freshly grated Parmesan cheese, to serve

Place the broccoli in a steamer and cook over boiling water for 5 minutes. Add the baby corn cobs and cook for a further 5 minutes. Alternatively, cook the vegetables for the same time in the minimum of boiling water; they have a better flavor if they are steamed.

Melt the butter or heat the oil in a large saucepan. Add the onion and bacon, and cook, stirring often, until both are cooked. Stir in the flour and a little seasoning, then add the sherry and stock. Stir in the broccoli and corn. Bring to a boil, reduce the heat and cover the pan. Simmer for 5 minutes. Taste for seasoning.

Serve the vegetables and their sauce tossed into pasta. Offer Parmesan cheese and extra ground pepper at the table.

Pumpkin Sauce

SERVES 4

3 tablespoons olive oil

2 large onions, chopped

1 garlic clove, crushed

1 bay leaf

2 tablespoons chopped sage

1 teaspoon dried marjoram

2 pounds pumpkin, seeded, peeled and cubed

salt and freshly ground black pepper

4 ounces button mushrooms, sliced

2 × 14-ounce oz cans chopped tomatoes

2 tablespoons chopped parsley

freshly grated Parmesan cheese, to serve

Heat the oil in a large saucepan. Add the onions, garlic, bay leaf, sage and marjoram. Cook, stirring, for 5 minutes, then add the pumpkin and mix well. Sprinkle in seasoning and continue to cook, stirring often, for 5 minutes. Stir in the mushrooms and tomatoes, heat until simmering and cover the pan. Cook gently for 35–40 minutes, until the pumpkin is tender but not mushy.

Stir in the parsley and taste for seasoning before serving, ladled over noodles or shapes. Offer Parmesan cheese with the pumpkin sauce and pasta.

Bell Pepper Sauce

SERVES 4–6

4 tablespoons olive oil

2 garlic cloves, finely chopped

8 ounces rindless bacon slices, diced

1 onion, halved and thinly sliced

2 red bell peppers, seeded, quartered lengthways and cut in strips

2 green bell peppers, seeded, quartered lengthways and cut in strips

¼ cup pine nuts

6 tablespoons raisins

salt and freshly ground black pepper

⅔ cup dry sherry

Heat the oil in a large skillet. Add the garlic, bacon, onion and red and green bell peppers. Cook, stirring often, for 5 minutes. Stir in the pine nuts and raisins with plenty of seasoning, then continue to cook, stirring occasionally, for 15 minutes.

Pour in the sherry and bring to a boil. Boil for 3 minutes. Taste and adjust the seasoning before pouring the sauce over the pasta. Toss well and serve at once.

Wonderful Mushroom Sauce

Look out for dried mushrooms in Italian and Eastern European delicatessens. This rich sauce, combining dried and fresh mushrooms, is delicious with plain noodles.

SERVES 4

2 whole dried mushrooms
⅔ cup boiling water
¼ stick (2 tablespoons) butter
1 tablespoon olive oil
½ small onion, finely chopped
1 bay leaf
12 ounces button mushrooms, sliced
½ cup dry sherry
salt and freshly ground black pepper
12 ounces oyster mushrooms
1¼ cups light cream
3 tablespoons chopped parsley
1 tablespoon lemon juice

Place the dried mushrooms in a small bowl and add the boiling water. Put a saucer on the mushrooms to keep them submerged and leave to soak for 15 minutes. Place the mushrooms and the liquid in a small saucepan and simmer for 10 minutes, adding a little extra water if necessary. Drain, reserving the cooking liquor. Chop the mushrooms. Strain the liquor through a cheesecloth-lined strainer to remove any grit.

Heat the butter and oil in a skillet. Add the onion and bay leaf, then cook, stirring, for 5 minutes. Add the sliced mushrooms and continue to cook for 15–20 minutes. The mushrooms will give up their liquor and shrink: this stage is complete when all the liquid has evaporated, leaving the darkened mushrooms in the oil and butter, and it is important for a good flavor. Add the dried mushrooms and the strained liquid. Stir in the sherry and seasoning, then simmer for 5 minutes.

Add the oyster mushrooms and poach them in the sauce for 3 minutes, so that they are hot and lightly cooked. Stir in the cream, parsley and lemon juice. Heat gently without boiling. Taste for seasoning and serve ladled over fresh noodles.

Good Tomato Sauce

Good fresh pasta and a rich tomato sauce, topped with some freshly grated Parmesan cheese, is a simple yet splendid meal, particularly if there is a really fresh, crisp green salad as an accompaniment. This sauce also has many uses in baked dishes or with stuffed pasta.

MAKES ABOUT 3¾ CUPS
SERVES 4–6

2 tablespoons olive oil
1 large onion, chopped
1 carrot, chopped
1 celery stalk, chopped
1 garlic clove, crushed
1 bay leaf
2 thyme sprigs
4 parsley sprigs
1 tablespoon all-purpose flour
2 tablespoons tomato paste
2 pounds ripe tomatoes, roughly chopped
1 tablespoon superfine sugar
⅔ cup dry red wine
salt and freshly ground black pepper
freshly grated Parmesan cheese, to serve

Heat the oil in a large, heavy-based saucepan. Add the onion, carrot, celery, garlic, bay leaf, thyme and parsley. Cook, stirring, for 10 minutes, until the onion is softened slightly but not browned.

Stir in the flour and tomato paste. Then add the tomatoes and sugar and stir in the wine. Add some seasoning, bring to a boil and give the sauce a good stir. Reduce the heat, cover the pan and leave to simmer for 1 hour.

Remove the bay leaf and herb sprigs, then purée the sauce in a blender and press it through a strainer to remove the seeds. Reheat and taste for seasoning before serving. Ladle the sauce over pasta and top with Parmesan cheese to taste.

Pesto

This is a wonderfully aromatic sauce based on basil. Grow a large pot of basil especially for the purpose of making pesto, or buy several pots of the growing herb (if you plant the roots and shoots from the base of such pots they will grow into large, healthy plants). Although pesto is traditionally made by pounding all the ingredients using a pestle and mortar, a food processor or blender is more or less essential for the busy cook. If you do not have either, then work in far smaller quantities than those given below.

MAKES ABOUT 2½ CUPS

6 ounces fresh Parmesan cheese, rind removed
4 ounces pine nuts
4 garlic cloves
2 cups basil sprigs (soft stems and leaves only, discard tough stalks before weighing)
1½–2 cups good-quality virgin olive oil
salt and freshly ground black pepper

Break the Parmesan into small pieces and place in the food processor with the pine nuts and garlic. Process the mixture until the Parmesan is finely crumbled. Add the basil and continue processing until the herb is chopped and the mixture begins to clump together into a coarse, bright green paste.

Add a little of the olive oil and process the mixture until it is incorporated, then gradually trickle in the remaining olive oil. Add enough to make a thin, pouring paste. Add seasoning to taste.

If using a blender, process the mixture in batches. The oil does not form a mayonnaise-like liaison: it will separate on standing and the paste has to be stirred again. Mix all the batches together at the end so that the ingredients are combined in the correct proportions.

Transfer the pesto to a clean screw-top jar and store it in the refrigerator. The oil acts as a preservative and the pesto will keep for several months if stored in an airtight container in the refrigerator. Stir it well before using.

Top individual portions of pasta with a couple of spoonfuls of pesto, then toss together and eat at once – delicious!

COOK'S TIP

If you are making a large batch of pesto for storing, sterilize the jars and their lids in a proprietary brand of sterilizing solution (from pharmacies; used for babies' bottles or for home brewing), then rinse with boiling water and allow to dry by draining. Leave the jars upside down until you fill them with pesto.

LEFT
Tomatoes and grapes on a courtyard table . . . wonderful ingredients for fresh pasta recipes.

Béchamel Sauce

Well-cooked, good-quality pasta makes a delicious meal with the minimum of additions: in the Italian kitchen that means olive oil and garlic or butter with Parmesan; to the traditional American or British cook a good milk-based sauce is popular too. Béchamel is a basic milk sauce which is lightly flavored with bay and mace: it is used in a variety of pasta dishes, notably as the topping for baked lasagne.

MAKES ABOUT 2½ CUPS

1 thick onion slice
1 bay leaf
1 mace blade
2 parsley sprigs
2½ cups milk
3 tablespoons butter
⅓ cup all-purpose flour
salt and freshly ground white or black pepper

Place the onion, bay leaf, mace and parsley in a saucepan. Add the milk and heat slowly until just boiling. Remove from the heat, cover and leave for 45 minutes.

Strain the milk into a jug or bowl. Wash the saucepan, then melt the butter and stir in the flour. Slowly pour in the milk, stirring all the time. Continue stirring until the sauce boils, then reduce the heat, if necessary, so that it just simmers. Cook for 3 minutes, stirring occasionally. Add seasoning to taste.

If the sauce is not used straightaway, lay a piece of dampened waxed paper directly on its surface to prevent a skin forming.

Variations

Any one of the following may be mixed with freshly cooked pasta and served as a light meal. A gratin topping may be added by sprinkling the sauced pasta with ½ cup fresh breadcrumbs mixed with 2 tablespoons freshly grated Parmesan cheese and browning under the broiler.

Cheese Sauce Stir in 1 cup grated sharp Cheddar cheese and 4 tablespoons freshly grated Parmesan cheese after the sauce has simmered.

Egg Sauce Hard-cook and roughly chop 6 eggs, then mix them into the cooked sauce. Add 1 tablespoon chopped tarragon or parsley, or 2 tablespoons chopped dill, if liked.

Mushroom Sauce Add 8 ounces sliced button mushrooms before the final simmering.

Onion Sauce Finely chop 2 large onions. Cook them in the butter for about 20 minutes, stirring often, until they are softened. Do not allow the onions to brown but do make sure that they are well cooked, otherwise the sauce will be inferior. Stir in the flour and continue as above.

Tuna Sauce Drain a 7-ounce can of tuna. Flake the fish and add it to the sauce before the final simmering. Add 2 tablespoons chopped parsley and 1 tablespoon chopped capers.

Tuna may be added to mushroom sauce, or an onion sauce may be prepared, then both mushrooms and tuna added. The oil from the can may be used instead of butter; brine may be added to the sauce with milk.

White Wine Sauce

MAKES 2½ CUPS

½ stick (¼ cup) butter

1 small onion, finely chopped

1 bay leaf

2 parsley sprigs with long stalks

2 ounces button mushrooms, thinly sliced

⅓ cup all-purpose flour

1¼ cups dry white wine

⅔ cup stock (chicken, vegetable or fish, depending on the dish)

salt and freshly ground white or black pepper

1¼ cups light cream

Melt the butter in a saucepan. Add the onion, bay leaf and parsley, then cook, stirring often, for 15 minutes, until the onion is softened slightly but not browned. Stir in the mushrooms, then stir in the flour. Gradually stir in the white wine and stock, then bring to a boil. The sauce will be too thick at this stage. Cover the pan tightly and allow the sauce to cook very gently for 15 minutes.

Add seasoning and beat the sauce well. Remove the bay leaf and parsley sprigs. Stir in the cream and heat gently without boiling.

BELOW
Vines growing at Monte Reggiano, Italy.

HOT CREATIONS
Timbales, Molds and Bakes

This is one of the chapters which points out the versatility
of pasta, particularly when the dough is homemade
and ready to roll to any shape or size required. The majority
of these recipes are excellent for preparing ahead, so
glance through these pages if you are looking for
an idea next time you are cooking for friends.
Although cooked pasta does not freeze well as a separate ingredient, prepared
layered dishes with sauce are terrific freezer candidates. If you are planning on
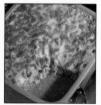 *freezing any of the dishes, remember that the freezer life of*
the finished dish is only as long as the shortest recommended time
for the ingredients included in it. If that sounds rather confusing,
a classic example is bacon which has a short freezer life and
does go rancid, spoiling the flavor of a dish or sauce.
Whether you are looking for a hearty hotpot or an elegant first course, I am
sure you will find something in the pages which follow.

Seafood Darioles

SERVES 4

3 ounces pasta dough (page 14), rolled out and cut into small squares

butter for greasing

⅔ cup Cheese Sauce (page 58)

4 ounces plaice fillet, skinned and chopped

4 ounces peeled cooked shrimp, thawed if frozen, chopped

1 tablespoon chopped parsley

2 tablespoons snipped chives

salt and freshly ground black pepper

1 egg, beaten

2 hard-cooked eggs

⅔ cup mayonnaise

3 tablespoons light cream

1 tablespoon chopped dill

dill or parsley and chives, to garnish

Cook the pasta in boiling salted water for 3 minutes, then drain. Set the oven at 350°F. Butter 4 dariole molds and line their bases with nonstick bakers' parchment. Stand the molds on a baking sheet.

Mix the pasta with the sauce. Add the fish, shrimp, parsley, chives, seasoning and beaten egg. Stir the mixture to make sure the ingredients are well combined, then divide it between the molds. Cover with nonstick bakers' parchment and bake for 30 minutes.

Meanwhile, finely chop the hard-cooked eggs and mix them with the mayonnaise. Add seasoning to taste, then stir in the cream and dill. Slide a fine knife blade around the inside of each mold, then invert them on individual plates. Remove the nonstick bakers' parchment and spoon a little of the egg sauce beside each mold; offer the rest of the sauce separately. Garnish with herbs and serve at once.

BELOW
Fishing boats from the Mediterranean Sea, which provide squid, sardines, swordfish and shrimp among their catches.

Salmon and Pasta Timbales

SERVES 4

2 ounces turmeric-flavored pasta dough (page 15)	2 ounces ricotta cheese, strained
salt and freshly ground black pepper	salt and freshly ground black pepper
1 7-ounce can salmon	1 egg, separated
1 cup fresh white bread crumbs	**To garnish**
1 tablespoon finely chopped scallion	basil or parsley sprigs
3 basil sprigs, finely shredded, or 1 tablespoon parsley	halved lemon slices

Roll out the pasta very thinly. Take a ramekin dish and cut a paper pattern of the base or find a round cutter to fit. Grease and base-line the ramekins with nonstick bakers' parchment. Cut 12 circles of pasta, then cook them in boiling salted water for 3 minutes. Drain the circles and place a circle of pasta in the bottom of each ramekin. Lay the remaining pasta out on paper towels. Set the oven at 350°F.

Drain the salmon, remove any skin and bone, then mash it. Mix with the bread crumbs, scallion, basil or parsley and ricotta cheese. Add seasoning and beat in the egg yolk. Whisk the egg white until stiff, then fold it into the salmon mixture. Divide the mixture roughly in half, then spoon one portion into the dishes, dividing it equally between them and spreading it neatly. Top each with a circle of pasta, then divide the remaining mixture between the dishes. Finally, top each with a circle of pasta. Stand on a baking sheet, cover with foil and bake for 25–30 minutes, or until the salmon mixture is set. It will also have risen.

Allow to stand for 2 minutes, then slide a knife around the inside of each ramekin. Invert the timbales on individual plates. Remove the nonstick bakers' parchment. Serve garnished with basil or parsley and lemon.

Seafood Lasagne

This is one of my favorite pasta dishes.

SERVES 6

12 ounces spinach-flavored pasta dough (page 15) or fresh lasagne verdi
2 tablespoons olive oil
1/4 stick (2 tablespoons) butter
1 onion, finely chopped
1 bay leaf
1/3 cup all-purpose flour
1 1/4 cups dry white wine
1 1/4 cups fish stock
4 ounces button mushrooms, sliced
salt and freshly ground black pepper
1 1/2 pounds white fish fillet, skinned and cut into chunks
8 ounces peeled cooked shrimp, thawed if frozen
1 pound mussels, cooked and shelled (page 40)
2 tablespoons chopped parsley
1 quantity Béchamel Sauce (page 58)
1/2 cup grated Cheddar cheese

Cut the rolled-out pasta into large squares (about 5 inches) or rectangular sheets. Lower the pieces of pasta one at a time into a large saucepan of boiling salted water. Bring back to a boil and cook for 3 minutes. Drain and rinse under cold water. Lay the pasta on double-thick paper towels.

Set the oven at 350°F. Heat the oil and butter in a saucepan and add the onion and bay leaf. Cook for 10 minutes, until the onion is softened slightly, then stir in the flour. Slowly pour in the wine and stock and bring to a boil, stirring all the time. Add the mushrooms and seasoning, then simmer for 10 minutes. Remove from the heat before stirring in the fish, shrimp, mussels and parsley. Layer this fish sauce and the lasagne in a large ovenproof dish, ending with a layer of lasagne. Pour the béchamel sauce evenly over the pasta, then sprinkle the cheese on top. Bake for 40–50 minutes, until golden-brown and bubbling hot.

Chicken and Ham Lasagne

This is easy and delicious! Turkey may be used instead of chicken – a great way of using up the Thanksgiving roast. Add any leftover stuffing to the sauce too.

SERVES 6–8

12 ounces spinach-flavored pasta dough (page 15) or fresh lasagne verdi

2 quantities Béchamel Sauce (page 58)

1½ cups diced cooked chicken

1½ cups diced cooked ham

4 ounces button mushrooms, chopped

6 scallions, chopped

2 tablespoons chopped parsley

1 tablespoon chopped sage

salt and freshly ground black pepper

¾ cup finely crumbled Monterey Jack or Colby cheese

paprika

½ cup fresh white bread crumbs

Prepare and cook the lasagne as for Classic Lasagne al Forno (page 64). Butter a 12–15 × 8-inch ovenproof dish and set the oven at 350°F.

Set aside a third of the béchamel sauce. Mix the chicken, ham, mushrooms, scallions, parsley and sage with the rest of the sauce. Taste for seasoning, then layer this sauce in the dish with the lasagne, ending with a layer of lasagne on top. Stir the cheese into the reserved sauce (it doesn't matter if the sauce is too cool for it to melt), then spread it over the top of the pasta. Sprinkle with a little paprika and top with the bread crumbs.

Bake for 40–50 minutes, until the topping is crisp and golden and the lasagne layers are bubbling hot.

COOK'S TIP

A mixture of crushed potato chips and a few finely chopped salted peanuts added to the bread crumbs makes a good topping.

RIGHT
Chicken and Ham Lasagne.

Classic Lasagne Al Forno

SERVES 6–8

12 ounces pasta dough (page 14) or fresh lasagne

salt and freshly ground black pepper

butter for greasing

1 quantity Rich Meat Ragout (page 47)

1½ quantities Béchamel Sauce (page 58)

¼ cup oz freshly grated Parmesan cheese

Cut the rolled-out pasta into large squares (about 5 inches) or rectangular sheets. Lower the pieces of pasta one at a time into a large saucepan of boiling salted water. Bring back to a boil and cook for 3 minutes. Drain and rinse under cold water. Lay the pasta on double-thick paper towels.

Set the oven at 350°F. Butter a large oblong ovenproof dish (about 12–15 × 8 inches). Ladle a little of the ragout into the dish and spread it out. Dot with a little of the béchamel sauce, then add a layer of pasta. Continue layering the meat, a little béchamel and pasta, ending with pasta. Do not include much béchamel between the layers as you need most of it to cover the top of the lasagne. Sprinkle the Parmesan over the top and bake the lasagne for 45–50 minutes, until golden-brown and bubbling hot.

Tagliatelle Turkey Bake

SERVES 4–6

2 tablespoons olive oil

1 onion, chopped

1 garlic clove, crushed

1 green bell pepper, seeded and diced

1 teaspoon dried marjoram

2½ cups diced cooked turkey

4 ounces mushrooms, thinly sliced

1 14-ounce can chopped tomatoes

3 tablespoons chopped parsley

salt and freshly ground black pepper

1 pound tagliatelle, cooked

4 fresh basil sprigs

2½ cups Béchamel Sauce (page 58)

4 ounces mozzarella cheese, diced

2 tablespoons freshly grated Parmesan cheese

Set the oven at 400°F. Heat the oil in a large saucepan. Add the onion, garlic, green bell pepper and marjoram. Cook, stirring often, for 15– 20 minutes, until the onion is softened. Stir in the turkey, mushrooms, tomatoes, parsley and seasoning. Remove from the heat and mix in the tagliatelle. Spoon the mixture into an ovenproof dish and press the top down with the back of a metal spoon so the noodles are fairly flat.

Use scissors to shred the basil and soft stalks into the béchamel sauce. Taste for seasoning, then pour the sauce evenly over the pasta mixture. Mix the mozzarella and Parmesan, then sprinkle this over the sauce. Bake for 40–45 minutes, until the topping is browned.

Asparagus Roulades

Halve the quantities if you want to serve these as a light first course.

SERVES 4

½ quantity pasta dough (page 14)
butter for greasing
½ cup cream cheese
4 tablespoons freshly grated Parmesan cheese
2 tablespoons snipped chives
½ cup fresh bread crumbs
salt and freshly ground black pepper
32 fine asparagus stalks, lightly cooked (page 24)
1 quantity Béchamel Sauce (page 58)

Roll out the pasta into a long sheet, slightly larger than 10 × 20 inches. (If it is more practical, roll out the dough in two batches.) Trim the dough neatly, cut it in half lengthways, then across at 8 equal intervals. This will make 16 rectangles measuring 5 × 2½ inches. Cook these in boiling salted water for 3 minutes, drain, rinse in cold water and lay out on double-thick paper towels.

Set the oven at 400°F. Butter an ovenproof dish. Mix the cream cheese, half the Parmesan, the chives and bread crumbs. Add a little seasoning. Spread or dot a little of the cheese mixture over a piece of pasta, then lay a couple of asparagus stalks on top and roll the pasta over to enclose them. Lay in the dish with the join in the pasta downward. Fill all the pasta in the same way.

Pour the béchamel sauce over the pasta and sprinkle with the remaining Parmesan. Bake for 20–25 minutes, until bubbling hot and lightly browned on top.

Spiced Squash and Pasta Bake

This is also a good recipe for pumpkin. Buy only good-quality curry powder prepared by a reputable manufacturer as the cheaper unknown brands can be revolting.

SERVES 4

¼ stick (2 tablespoons) butter

1 onion, chopped

1 garlic clove, crushed

1½ pounds summer squash, seeded, peeled and cut in small cubes

1 teaspoon mild curry powder

8 ounces button mushrooms, sliced

¼ cup ground almonds

1 tablespoon all-purpose flour

1¼ cups coconut milk (see Cook's Tip)

grated peel of 1 lime

salt and freshly ground black pepper

12 ounces pasta spirals, cooked

1¼ cups light cream

slivered almonds

Set the oven at 350°F. Melt the butter in a large saucepan. Add the onion and garlic and cook for 5 minutes, then stir in the squash, curry powder and mushrooms. Cook for 25–30 minutes, stirring often, until the squash is tender. Stir in the ground almonds and flour, then pour in the coconut milk, stirring all the time, and bring to simmering point. Remove from the heat and add the lime rind with seasoning to taste.

Mix the pasta with the cream and turn half of it into an ovenproof dish or casserole. Spread the pasta out in an even layer, then top with the squash mixture, then cover with the remaining pasta in an even layer. Sprinkle the almonds over the top and bake for 30 minutes, until lightly browned on top.

COOK'S TIP

Coconut milk can be made as follows: soak shredded or freshly grated coconut in boiling water, and cover for 30 minutes. Then squeeze out all the liquid, pressing the mixture with a spoon in a strainer. Alternatively, you can buy instant coconut milk powder and dilute it according to the package instructions.

Cauliflower and Stilton Terrine

SERVES 6

1 pound cauliflower
6 ounces blue Stilton cheese, finely crumbled
2 cups fresh white bread crumbs
8 scallions, finely chopped
1 tablespoon chopped sage
2/3 cup sour cream
4 tablespoons dry sherry
2 eggs
salt and freshly ground black pepper
freshly grated nutmeg
butter for greasing
1/2 quantity spinach-flavored pasta dough (page 15) or fresh lasagne verdi
Good Tomato Sauce (page 56), to serve

Cook the cauliflower in boiling water for 5 minutes, then drain well before chopping the flowerets. Mix the cauliflower, Stilton, bread crumbs, scallions, sage, sour cream, sherry and eggs. Add seasoning and a little nutmeg.

Set the oven at 350°F. Prepare a bain marie and butter a 2-pound loaf pan. Cut the fresh pasta into wide strips which are long enough to line the pan widthways and overhang the sides. Cook the pasta for 3 minutes, drain and rinse in cold water, then lay out to dry on double-thick paper towels.

Line the pan completely with bands of pasta, overlapping them neatly. If bought fresh lasagne is not long enough, then overlap strips as you do need some pasta overhanging the rim of the pan. Spread a layer of cauliflower mixture in the base of the pan, then cover with a layer of pasta, cutting it to fit neatly and overlapping pieces as necessary. Continue layering cauliflower mixture and pasta until the pan is full, ending with cauliflower mixture.

Fold the ends of the pasta over. Add a final layer of pasta to cover the top of the terrine neatly. Generously butter a piece of greaseproof paper and lay it on top of the pasta. Cover with foil, sealing it well around the edges of the pan. Stand the pan in the bain marie and bake it for 1½ hours, until the mixture is firm to the touch and cooked through. Allow to stand for 5 minutes after cooking.

Slide a palette knife between the pasta and the pan, then invert the terrine on a flat platter. Use a serrated knife to cut the terrine into thick slices and serve with tomato sauce.

Pork and Pasta Rolls

SERVES 4

1 pound ground pork
1 cup fresh white bread crumbs
1 onion, finely chopped
1 tablespoon chopped rosemary
2 tablespoons chopped parsley
2 eggs, beaten
salt and freshly ground black pepper
½ quantity carrot-flavored pasta dough (page 15)
1¼ cups dry cider
2½ cups chicken stock
3 tablespoons butter
2 tablespoons all-purpose flour
rosemary sprigs, to garnish (optional)

Mix the pork, bread crumbs, onion, rosemary, parsley and half the beaten egg. Add plenty of seasoning and pound the mixture until all the ingredients are thoroughly combined.

Roll out the dough into a rectangle measuring slightly larger than 17 × 10 inches. Trim the edges, then brush the pasta with beaten egg. Spread the meat mixture all over the roll, leaving a narrow border around the edge. Roll up the pasta from the long end. Seal the end of the roll with more beaten egg and press it down on the roll with a blunt knife.

Set the oven at 350°F. Prepare a large saucepan of boiling water. Cut the roll in half or quarters, depending on the size of the saucepan. Carefully lower the pieces of roll into the water and simmer for 3 minutes. Wrapping a couple of bands of folded foil around the roll helps with lowering it into the water and lifting it out again; otherwise use a large fish slice and slotted spoon to drain the pieces of roll. Cut the roll into 16 slices and place them in an ovenproof casserole.

Heat the cider and stock together, then pour them over the rolls, cover and bake for 1 hour. Meanwhile, beat the butter into the flour. Transfer the cooked rolls to a serving dish or individual plates and keep hot. Bring the cooking juices to a boil in a saucepan, then gradually whisk in the butter and flour paste. Boil for 3 minutes, then taste for seasoning. Spoon a little of the sauce over the rolls and offer the rest separately. Garnish with fresh rosemary sprigs if you like.

RIGHT
One of the most famous views in Italy – the Brunelleschi dome of Florence cathedral.

Turkey and Lasagne Ring

SERVES 4

4 ounces spinach-flavored pasta dough (page 15) or fresh lasagne verdi

4 ounces pasta dough (page 14) or fresh lasagne

2 tablespoons oil

1 pound leeks, chopped

3 cups diced turkey

1 cooking apple, peeled, cored and chopped

1 cup fresh bread crumbs

2 tablespoons chopped sage

salt and freshly ground black pepper

1 egg

Mushroom Sauce (page 58) to serve

Roll out both doughs separately and cut them into wide bands, or lasagne, long enough to line a 1-quart ring pan. Cook the lasagne in boiling salted water for 3 minutes, then drain and rinse it under cold water. Lay out on double-thick paper towels.

Heat the oil in a large saucepan. Add the leeks and cook for about 15 minutes, until they are greatly reduced in volume and softened. Remove from the heat. Mix in the turkey, apple, bread crumbs, sage, plenty of seasoning and egg. Make sure the ingredients are thoroughly combined.

Set the oven at 350°F. Grease a 1-quart ring pan. Line it with lasagne, alternating the verdi and plain sheets, and leaving the pasta overlapping the rim of the pan. Fill with the turkey mixture, then fold the ends of the lasagne over neatly. Cover with greased foil and bake for 1 hour. Check that the turkey mixture is cooked through by inserting the point of a knife into the middle of it and taking out a small portion.

Invert the ring on a platter. Cut into slices to serve and offer mushroom sauce to pour over individual portions.

COOK'S TIP

Fill the middle of the ring with vegetables, such as sautéed zucchini, glazed carrots or green beans sautéed with red bell peppers and onions.

71

Lamb and Pasta Hotpot

This is a heart-warming winter stew! Beef, pork or bacon may all be used instead of lamb. Offer some crusty bread to mop up the juices.

SERVES 4

1 tablespoon oil

1¼ pounds lean boneless lamb, cubed

1 onion, chopped

2 carrots, diced

2 rosemary sprigs

salt and freshly ground black pepper

2½ cups light beer

2½ cups water

8 ounces frozen peas

1 pound pasta spirals

⅔ cup sour cream

paprika

croûtons, to serve

Heat the oil in a large flameproof casserole or heavy-based saucepan. Add the lamb and brown the cubes all over. Stir in the onion, carrots, rosemary sprigs and seasoning. Cook, stirring, for a few minutes, then add the beer and water. Bring just to a boil, reduce the heat and cover the pan. Leave the hotpot to simmer for 1¼ hours, stirring occasionally until the lamb is tender and the cooking liquor is well flavored.

Taste for seasoning, then add the peas. Bring back to a boil, reduce the heat and cover the pot. Simmer for 15 minutes. Add the pasta, stir well, then bring back to a boil. Partially cover the pan and cook for 5 minutes, only allowing the hotpot to boil very slowly.

Top individual portions of the hotpot with sour cream and sprinkle with paprika. Sprinkle with croûtons and serve piping hot.

Venison on a Bed of Pasta

Venison is delicious in this lightly spiced, creamy sauce. For a cheaper alternative, prepare a braising piece of beef, such as chuck, in the same way. Ask the butcher to truss the meat neatly so that it stays in good shape during cooking. Serve with green beans and glazed carrot strips.

SERVES 6

1 3-pound boneless leg of venison
1 onion, thinly sliced
1 carrot, diced
1 tablespoon coriander seeds, coarsely crushed
1 teaspoon green peppercorns, crushed
1 bay leaf
1 bottle dry white wine
2 tablespoons pistachio oil
2 tablespoons oil
¾ cup diced bacon
salt and freshly ground black pepper
¾ cup roughly chopped prunes
4 ounces crimini mushrooms, sliced
3 tablespoons butter
¼ cup all-purpose flour
1 pound noodles
1¼ cups sour cream

Place the venison in a mixing bowl. Add the onion, carrot, coriander seeds, peppercorns and bay leaf. Pour the wine over the meat, then trickle the pistachio oil over. Cover and leave to marinate in the refrigerator for 24 hours, turning the meat in the marinade as often as possible.

Heat the oil in a large flameproof casserole or heavy-based saucepan. Brown the piece of venison very well on all sides. Add the bacon, cook for 2–3 minutes, then add all the marinade. Add plenty of seasoning and pour in enough water to cover two-thirds the venison. Bring just to the boil, reduce the heat and cover with a close-fitting lid. Simmer for 1½ hours, then carefully turn the venison. Add the prunes and mushrooms and cook for a further 1¼ hours. Cream the butter and flour to a smooth paste and set aside.

Add the noodles to the pan. Bring back to a boil, then reduce the heat and simmer for a further 10 minutes. Lift the venison from the pan. Use a slotted spoon to transfer the noodles to a heated serving dish. Cover and keep hot. Boil the cooking liquid rapidly in the open pan until it is reduced to about 1¾ cups.

Meanwhile, carve the venison and arrange it on top of the noodles. Cover and keep hot. Whisk the flour paste into the sauce and boil for 2 minutes, whisking all the time. Remove from the heat, stir in the sour cream and taste for seasoning. Heat gently if necessary but do not boil. Pour some of the sauce over the meat and noodles and offer the rest separately.

CHAPTER FIVE

STUFFED PASTA
Fillings For Flavor

Homemade stuffed pasta really is worth the effort for the quality is evident in the texture of the filling as well as in the flavors. Although it can take a while to get

started, once you have a "filling, shaping and sealing" production line going, and you have got the feel for your dough, it is surprising how relaxing stuffing pasta can be . . . rather like eating it, in fact.

Before you start to pile up the finished pasta shapes, prepare a large platter or roasting pan for holding them by dusting it with flour. Keep the finished pasta lightly dusted with flour if you have to pile it up, otherwise the shapes will stick together and break.

If the dough dries out as you are filling cut pieces it will be difficult to handle and seal, so keep it loosely covered with plastic

wrap. Do not be over-ambitious about the quantity of filling which will fit into small pieces of pasta. Most of the fillings are well seasoned, so a little gives a lot of flavor whereas too much will only split the dough casing during cooking. Brush the dough edges with a little egg but do not make them too wet: not only does this make filling the dough a messy task, it also causes the two edges to slip apart. Lastly, remember that the cooking time for stuffed pasta shapes such as ravioli depends on the type of filling – raw meat filling takes longer to cook through than a cooked mixture does.

Tuna Triangles

SERVES 6–8

1 7-ounce can tuna, drained

2 tablespoons finely chopped scallions

1 garlic clove, crushed

1 cup fresh white bread crumbs

grated peel of 1/2 lemon

4 tablespoons freshly grated Parmesan cheese

salt and freshly ground black pepper

about 3 tablespoons milk

2/3 quantity pasta dough (page 14)

1 egg, beaten

Good Tomato Sauce (page 56),
White Wine Sauce (page 59),
Cheese Sauce (page 58) or Mushroom Sauce (page 58)

freshly grated Parmesan cheese, to serve

Mash the tuna, then mix in the scallions, garlic and bread crumbs. Add the lemon peel, Parmesan cheese and seasoning to taste. Mix in just enough milk to bind the mixture.

Roll out half the pasta dough into a 12½-inch square. Cut it into 5 × 2½-inch strips, then cut these across into squares. Brush a square of dough with a little egg. Place a little tuna mixture in the center of the dough, then fold it in half in a triangular shape. Pinch the edges together well to seal in the filling. Repeat with the remainder of the rolled dough, then do the same with the second half.

Bring a large saucepan of salted water to a boil. Add the triangles and bring the water back to a boil. Do not let the water boil too rapidly or the pasta may burst: keep it just boiling steadily. Cook for 4–5 minutes, then drain well.

Serve the triangles with any one of the sauces listed and offer Parmesan cheese at the table.

Savory Sardine Cannelloni

An inexpensive dish for a midweek meal. The sardine and cheese mixture is also good for filling ravioli or tortellini.

SERVES 4

¹⁄₃ quantity pasta dough (page 14)

2 × 4-ounce cans sardines in oil

1 onion, chopped

1 garlic clove, crushed

1¹⁄₂ cups fresh white bread crumbs

4 ounces button mushrooms, chopped

¹⁄₂ cup low-fat soft cheese

1 cup grated Cheddar cheese

grated peel and juice of 1 lemon

salt and freshly ground black pepper

butter for greasing

1 quantity Good Tomato Sauce (page 56)

Roll out the pasta into a thin 16-inch square. Cut it into 4 × 4-inch wide strips, then cut the strips across to make 16 squares. Bring a large pan of salted water to a boil and cook the pieces of pasta, a few at a time if necessary, for 3 minutes. Drain and rinse under cold water, then lay out on double-thick paper towels.

Pour the oil from the sardines into a small saucepan. Add the onion and garlic, then cook, stirring often, for 10 minutes. Remove from the heat. Mash the sardines and add them to the onion and garlic. Mix in the bread crumbs, mushrooms, soft cheese, three-quarters of the Cheddar cheese, the lemon peel and juice, and seasoning to taste.

Set the oven at 400°F. Butter an ovenproof dish. Place some of the sardine mixture on a piece of pasta, then roll it up into a neat tube and place in the dish with the end of the roll underneath. Repeat with the remaining pasta and filling. Ladle the tomato sauce over the cannelloni, then sprinkle with the remaining cheese. Bake for 25–30 minutes, until the cheese has melted and browned. Serve at once.

Chicken Tortellini

SERVES 6–8

1½ cups ground cooked chicken
½ cup fresh white bread crumbs
2 tablespoons very finely chopped onion
1 tablespoon chopped sage
2 tablespoons chopped parsley
4 tablespoons light cream or milk
salt and freshly ground black pepper
⅔ quantity pasta dough (page 14)
1 egg, beaten
White Wine Sauce (page 59) or Good Tomato Sauce (page 56)
freshly grated Parmesan cheese, to serve

Mix the chicken, bread crumbs, onion, sage, parsley and cream or milk. Add seasoning and pound the mixture with the spoon to insure all the ingredients are thoroughly combined.

Cut the pasta dough in half. Roll out one piece into a 12-inch square – it is a good idea to roll the dough nominally larger, then trim it neatly. Cut the dough into 6 × 2-inch strips, then cut across these to make 2-inch squares. Brush a square of dough with a little egg, then place a little of the chicken filling in the center of it. Seal two opposite corners together to make a triangular shape. Wrap the long side of the triangle around your fingertip and pinch the corners together to make a miter shape (or bishop's hat shape). Continue filling and sealing the tortellini, then roll out the second portion of dough and repeat the process. Do not overfill the tortellini or they will burst during cooking.

Bring a large saucepan of salted water to a boil. Add the tortellini and bring the water back to a boil. Do not boil the pasta too rapidly or they will split. Cook for 5 minutes, then drain thoroughly. Serve the tortellini with White Wine Sauce or Good Tomato Sauce and offer Parmesan cheese at the table.

Alternative Serving Ideas

▌ Toss the tortellini in hot melted butter and Parmesan cheese.

▌ Serve with Béchamel Sauce (page 58).

▌ Serve with Pesto (page 57).

▌ Serve the tortellini in soup, such as consommé or chicken broth.

Pork and Rosemary Ravioli

Depending on where you are in Italy, ravioli may be square or round. Round filled pasta may also be referred to as agnolotti, again according to regional preferences and traditions.

SERVES 12

2 tablespoons olive oil

1 onion, finely chopped

2 garlic cloves, crushed

4 juniper berries, crushed

1 tablespoon chopped rosemary

1/2 teaspoon ground mace

12 ounces lean ground pork

1 cup fresh white bread crumbs

1/2 cup chopped mushrooms

salt and freshly ground black pepper

2 eggs

1 quantity pasta dough (page 14)

To serve

White Wine Sauce (page 59)

4 ounces button mushrooms, thinly sliced

2 tablespoons chopped parsley

freshly grated Parmesan cheese

Heat the oil in a saucepan. Add the onion, garlic and juniper berries. Cook, stirring, for 15 minutes, or until the onion is softened. Stir in the rosemary, mace, pork, bread crumbs, mushrooms and plenty of seasoning. Add 1 egg and thoroughly mix the ingredients, pounding them with the back of the spoon. Beat the remaining egg.

Roll out half the pasta dough slightly larger than a 18-inch square. Use a 2-inch round cutter to stamp out circles of pasta, dipping the cutter in flour occasionally so that it cuts the dough cleanly. The best way to do this is to stamp all the circles close together in neat lines in the dough, then lift away the unwanted trimmings when the whole sheet is stamped into circles. You should have about 80 circles. Keep the circles which are not actually being used covered with plastic wrap while you fill the ravioli. Brush a circle of dough with egg, then place some of the meat mixture on it and cover with a second circle of dough. Pinch the edges of the dough together to seal in the filling. Fill all the ravioli, then roll out the remaining dough and make a second batch.

Cook the ravioli in a large saucepan of boiling water, allowing 15 minutes once the water has come back to a boil. Do this in batches if necessary, then drain the pasta.

Make the sauce but do not add the cream. Add the mushrooms and simmer for 5 minutes before stirring in the cream and parsley. Pour the sauce over the ravioli and serve with Parmesan cheese.

Beef Ravioli with Tomato Sauce

SERVES 6

1 tablespoon oil
½ onion, finely chopped
1 garlic clove, crushed
½ teaspoon dried marjoram
¼ teaspoon chopped thyme
¼ teaspoon ground coriander
salt and freshly ground black pepper
4 ounces finely ground sirloin steak
½ cup ground lean bacon
½ cup fresh white bread crumbs
1 egg, beaten
⅔ quantity pasta dough (page 14)
1 quantity Good Tomato Sauce (page 56)
freshly grated Parmesan cheese, to serve

Heat the oil in a small saucepan. Add the onion, garlic, marjoram, thyme, coriander and seasoning. Cook, stirring, for 5 minutes, then remove from the heat. Mix in the steak, bacon and bread crumbs. Add a little of the egg to bind the ingredients. Pound the mixture until thoroughly mixed.

Cut the pasta dough in half. Roll out one half into a rectangle measuring slightly larger than 14 × 10 inches. Trim the edges of the dough neatly. Cover the rolled-out dough with plastic wrap, then roll out the second portion of dough in the same way but do not bother to trim the edges this time, as a little more dough is needed to cover the stuffing.

Dot small balls of the meat mixture in even lines over the neat rectangle of pasta dough, leaving a gap of about ¾ inch between them. You should have 34–36 ravioli. Whisk a little water into the remaining beaten egg, to make it go further if necessary, then brush it over the dough between the mounds of meat. Carefully lay the second sheet of dough over the top. Starting at one end, seal the dough around the meat, carefully pressing out the air and flattening the meat slightly to seal the packages. Use a sharp knife or pastry wheel to trim the pasta edges and cut between the mounds of meat. Make sure the ravioli are neat and flour them slightly, if necessary, to prevent them sticking together.

Bring a large saucepan of salted water to a boil. Reduce the heat slightly so that it is not bubbling too rapidly and add the ravioli. Keep the water just boiling steadily and cook the ravioli for 10–15 minutes. Meanwhile, heat the tomato sauce. Drain the ravioli, turn them into a serving dish and pour the tomato sauce over them. Mix lightly before serving with Parmesan cheese.

Walnut Cheese Ravioli

SERVES 6

2 tablespoons olive oil
1 small onion, finely chopped
1 garlic clove, crushed
1 cup finely chopped walnuts
4 ounces ricotta cheese
3 ounces gruyère cheese
2 tablespoons freshly grated Parmesan cheese
6 basil sprigs, finely shredded
1 cup fresh white bread crumbs
salt and freshly ground black pepper
⅔ quantity pasta dough (page 14)
1 egg, beaten
White Wine Sauce (page 59) or hot melted butter, to serve

Heat the oil in a small saucepan. Add the onion and garlic and cook for 15 minutes, until the onion is softened but not browned. Remove from the heat, then stir in the walnuts, ricotta, gruyère, Parmesan cheese, basil and bread crumbs. Add seasoning to taste and mix the ingredients thoroughly.

Make the ravioli as for the Beef Ravioli with Tomato Sauce (page 79), making sure the mixture is well sealed in the dough. Cook the ravioli for 5 minutes in water which is just boiling, as the cheese filling does not take as long to cook through as the raw beef filling. Drain and serve with White Wine Sauce or simply with butter and pepper.

Spinach and Ricotta Tortellini

SERVES 6–8

6 ounces fresh spinach, trimmed and cooked

4 ounces ricotta cheese

4 tablespoons freshly grated Parmesan cheese

½ cup fresh white bread crumbs

pinch of dried thyme

1 teaspoon dried marjoram

a little freshly grated nutmeg

salt and freshly ground black pepper

⅔ quantity pasta dough (page 14)

1 egg, beaten

Make sure the spinach is thoroughly drained, then chop it finely. Mix it with the ricotta, Parmesan, bread crumbs and herbs. Add a little nutmeg and seasoning to taste.

Use the dough and beaten egg to make and fill the tortellini, following the instructions for Chicken Tortellini (page 77). Cook and serve the tortellini in the same way.

Harvest Moons

These are unusual, filling and nutritious – good if you like spiced food and ideal for a vegetarian lunch.

SERVES 4

1 tablespoon oil
1/2 small onion, chopped
1/2 small carrot, chopped
1 garlic clove, crushed
1 teaspoon cumin seeds
1 teaspoon ground coriander

1/2 × 14-ounce can chick peas, drained
1 tomato, peeled and chopped
2 teaspoons chopped cilantro leaves
salt and freshly ground black pepper
1/2 quantity turmeric-flavored pasta dough (page 15)
1 egg, beaten
1/2 stick (2 tablespoons) lightly salted butter
1/2 cucumber, peeled and diced
2 tablespoons chopped mint

Heat the oil in a small saucepan. Add the onion, carrot, garlic and cumin seeds. Cook, stirring often, for 10 minutes. Stir in the coriander and cook for 2 minutes, then remove the pan from the heat. Roughly mash the chick peas – they should not be completely smooth. Stir the chick peas into the onion mixture, then add the tomatoes, chopped cilantro and seasoning to taste.

Roll out the pasta dough into a 18-inch square. Use a 2-inch round cutter to stamp out circles of pasta, dipping the cutter in flour occasionally so that it cuts the dough cleanly. The best way to do this is to stamp all the circles close together in neat lines in the dough, then lift away the unwanted trimmings when the whole sheet is stamped into circles. You should have about 80 circles. Keep the circles which are not actually being used covered with cling film while you fill some of them.

Brush a circle of dough with egg, then place some of the chick pea mixture on it. Fold the pasta in half to make a tiny moon-shaped turnover. Pinch the edges of the dough together to seal in the filling. Repeat with the remaining pasta circles. Cook the turnovers in boiling salted water, allowing 3–5 minutes after the water comes back to a boil.

While the pasta is cooking, heat the butter. Add the cucumber and mint and set aside over low heat. Turn the cooked pasta into a warmed serving dish and pour the butter and cucumber mixture over. Toss well, then serve at once.

Three-Cheese Cannelloni

Only good-quality Parmesan cheese is suitable for the filling in these cannelloni. Bought grated Parmesan, which is strong but lacking the sweetness of a good cheese, will taste too pungent. A fresh, crisp and extremely simple green salad is the perfect accompaniment to complement the richness of the cheese and tomato in the baked dish.

SERVES 4

⅓ quantity pasta dough (page 14)
8 ounces ricotta cheese
¾ cup freshly grated Parmesan cheese
2 cups fresh white bread crumbs
1 teaspoon dried oregano
1 bunch watercress, trimmed and chopped
salt and freshly ground black pepper
freshly grated nutmeg
butter for greasing
1 quantity Good Tomato Sauce (page 56)
6 ounces mozzarella cheese, thinly sliced
handful of basil sprigs

Roll out the pasta thinly into a 16-inch square. Cut it into 4 × 4-inch wide strips, then cut the strips across to make 16 squares. Bring a large pan of salted water to a boil and cook the pieces of pasta, a few at a time if necessary, for 3 minutes. Drain and rinse under cold water, then lay out on double-thick paper towels.

Mix the ricotta, Parmesan, bread crumbs, oregano and watercress. Add seasoning and a little grated nutmeg to taste, then stir the mixture to make sure all the ingredients are thoroughly combined.

Set the oven at 400°F. Butter an ovenproof dish. Place some of the cheese mixture on a piece of pasta, then roll it up into a neat tube and place in the dish with the end of the roll underneath. Repeat with the remaining pasta and filling. Ladle the tomato sauce over the cannelloni, then top with the mozzarella. Bake for 25–30 minutes, until the cheese has melted and browned. Use scissors to shred the basil leaves and soft stems and sprinkle over the cannelloni. Serve at once.

Eggplant Packages

Halve the quantities if you want to serve one package per person for a light main course or starter.

SERVES 4

2 small eggplants
salt and freshly ground black pepper
4–6 tablespoons olive oil
2 large slices lean cooked ham
8 sage leaves
8 ounces (8 small slices) dolcelatte cheese
⅔ quantity pasta dough (page 14)
2 large onions, thinly sliced
1 pound ripe tomatoes, peeled and sliced
½ cup soft cheese with garlic and herbs
1 cup fine dry white bread crumbs
4 tablespoons freshly grated Parmesan cheese

Trim the eggplants and cut eight slices. Layer these in a strainer with a little salt, place over a bowl, then leave to stand for 30 minutes. Rinse well and dry on paper towels.

Heat some olive oil in a skillet and brown the eggplants on both sides, adding more oil as necessary. Cut the ham into eight pieces. Sandwich the eggplant slices in pairs, placing a piece of ham, sage leaf and slice of dolcelatte between each pair.

Roll out half the dough into a 12-inch square. Cut this into 4 × 6-inch squares, boil for 3 minutes and dry on double-thick paper towels. Place an eggplant sandwich in the center of each square and fold the pasta over it to make a neat package. Repeat with the remaining pasta and eggplants.

Set the oven at 350°F. Heat any remaining olive oil. Add the onions and cook for 15–20 minutes, until softened. Spread the onions in the base of an ovenproof dish. Top with the tomatoes and season well. Arrange the eggplant packages on top, with the ends of the pasta dough underneath. Dot the tops of the packages with the soft cheese, spreading it slightly. Mix the bread crumbs and Parmesan, then sprinkle some over the top of each package. Cover with greased foil and bake for 20 minutes, then remove the foil and cook for a further 10 minutes.

RIGHT
A traditional shuttered house in Tuscany.

84

Cannelloni with Carrot and Zucchini

SERVES 4

⅓ quantity pasta dough (page 14)
3 tablespoons olive oil
1 onion, chopped
1 garlic clove, crushed
1½ cups grated carrot
¾ cup grated zucchini
1 cup fresh white bread crumbs
2 tomatoes, peeled and chopped
2 tablespoons chopped parsley
1 teaspoon dried marjoram
salt and freshly ground black pepper
1 quantity Cheese Sauce (page 58)
3 tablespoons dry white bread crumbs

Roll out the pasta thinly into a 16-inch square. Cut it into 4 × 4-inch wide strips, then cut the strips across four times to make 16 squares. Bring a large pan of salted water to a boil and cook the pieces of pasta, a few at a time if necessary, for 3 minutes. Drain and rinse under cold water, then lay out on double-thick paper towels.

Set the oven at 350°F. Heat the oil in a large saucepan. Add the onion and garlic and cook for 15 minutes, until the onion is softened but not browned. Stir in the carrots and continue to cook, stirring all the time, for a further 20 minutes, or until the carrots are tender. Regulate the heat to prevent the carrots from browning. Stir in the zucchini, cook for 2–3 minutes, then remove the pan from the heat. Add the bread crumbs, tomatoes, parsley, marjoram and seasoning to taste.

Place some of the vegetable mixture on a piece of pasta, then roll it up into a neat tube and place in the dish with the end of the roll underneath. Repeat with the remaining pasta and filling. Pour the cheese sauce over the cannelloni. Sprinkle the bread crumbs on top and bake for 40 minutes, until golden-brown.

CHAPTER SIX

PASTA COOL
The Freshest Salad Ideas

I hope the recipes in this chapter will inspire new enthusiasm for pasta salads. There seemed to be a culinary phase, no longer popular, when everyone made vast bowlfuls of either rice salad or pasta salad whenever a few friends gathered – a great idea it is too, but only if the pasta is perfectly "al dente," the other ingredients are complementary and the dressing brings the whole dish together.

I usually prefer pasta shapes in salads but I have also included a couple of ideas for noodles and spaghetti. Making a salad is a good way of using up any leftover pasta dough: cut out your own shapes using cutters or by cutting strips, then squares or diamond shapes. However, avoid ragged shapes and irregular offcuts which can be rather off-putting in a salad. If you do happen to have cooked too much pasta for a meal, turn the surplus into a salad for a picnic or a light lunch the following day.

Smoked Salmon and Pasta Cocktails

This turns a comparatively small quantity of smoked salmon into an attractive starter.

SERVES 4

4 ounces fresh pasta spirals

4 tablespoons mayonnaise

4 tablespoons sour cream

2 tablespoons snipped chives

salt and freshly ground black pepper

4 chicory leaves, roughly shredded

6 ounces smoked salmon, shredded

2 tablespoons chopped fresh dill

grated peel of 1/2 lemon

fresh dill sprigs, to garnish

4 lemon wedges, to serve

Cook the pasta in boiling salted water for 3 minutes. Drain and cool. Mix the mayonnaise, sour cream and chives with the pasta. Add seasoning to taste.

Arrange the chicory in four glass dishes, then divide the pasta between the dishes. Mix the smoked salmon with the dill and lemon peel, then arrange the shreds on top of the pasta. Garnish with dill sprigs. Serve lemon wedges with the cocktails so that their juice may be sprinkled over the smoked salmon.

Crab and Zucchini Salad

SERVES 4

8 ounces fresh pasta shapes

8 ounces small, young zucchini

6 scallions, chopped

6 basil sprigs

salt and freshly ground black pepper

2 tablespoons lemon juice

2 tablespoons olive oil

6 ounces crabmeat

4 eggs, hard-cooked

4 tablespoons chopped parsley

Cook the pasta in boiling salted water for 3 minutes. Drain well and place in a bowl. Trim and coarsely grate the zucchini, then add them to the pasta with the scallions. Use scissors to shred the basil leaves and soft stalk ends into the salad. Sprinkle in seasoning to taste and mix in the lemon juice. Add the olive oil and mix well. Arrange the mixture in a serving dish, leaving a hollow in the middle.

Flake the crabmeat. Chop the eggs and mix them with the crab. Fork in the parsley and seasoning to taste, then spoon the mixture in the middle of the pasta. Serve at once; if the salad is allowed to stand, the pasta and zucchini become watery.

Ham and Avocado Salad

SERVES 4

12 ounces fresh pasta shapes

2 tablespoons cider vinegar

1 teaspoon prepared wholegrain mustard

½ teaspoon superfine sugar

salt and freshly ground black pepper

6 tablespoons olive oil

1 pound lean cooked ham (in one piece), cubed

2 avocados

4 tablespoons snipped chives

½ cup walnuts, chopped

1 lettuce heart or ½ iceberg lettuce, shredded (optional)

Cook the pasta in boiling salted water for 3 minutes, then drain well. Meanwhile, mix the cider vinegar, mustard, superfine sugar and seasoning in a basin. Whisk the mixture until the sugar and salt have dissolved. Gradually whisk in the oil. Place the hot pasta into a dish and pour the dressing over it, then mix well.

Allow the pasta to cool slightly before mixing in the ham. Just before serving the salad, halve the avocados, remove their pits and quarter the halves lengthways. Remove the peel, then cut the flesh into chunks and mix them with the pasta. Mix in the chives and walnuts.

Arrange the salad on a base of shredded lettuce, if liked, and serve promptly. If the salad is allowed to stand, the avocado will discolor.

Smoked Mackerel Salad

This is simple, extremely well flavored and delicious for a summer lunch.   Serve crusty bread to complement the pasta.

SERVES 4

8 ounces fresh pasta shapes
½ stick (¼ cup) butter
1 cup fresh white bread crumbs
grated peel of 1 lemon
4 tablespoons chopped parsley
⅔ cup sour cream
4 tablespoons horseradish sauce
1 teaspoon finely chopped rosemary
4 scallions, chopped
salt and freshly ground black pepper
4 smoked mackerel fillets, skinned and coarsely flaked
2 tomatoes, peeled and chopped (see Cook's Tip, page 26)

Cook the pasta in boiling salted water for 3 minutes, then drain it and set it aside to cool. Melt the butter in a skillet, add the bread crumbs and fry them, stirring often, until they are crisp and golden.

Remove from the heat, stir in the lemon peel and 2 tablespoons of the parsley, and leave to cool.

Mix the sour cream, horseradish sauce, rosemary and scallions with the pasta. Toss the shapes well to coat them in the sauce, then add seasoning to taste. Lightly fork the smoked mackerel and remaining parsley into the pasta mixture, then spoon the salad into a shallow dish. Garnish with a neat line of chopped tomato and a couple of lines of the fried bread crumb mixture. Serve promptly after garnishing so that the bread crumbs are still crisp when eaten.

COOK'S TIP

The rosemary must be finely chopped, otherwise the spiky leaves are unpleasant. To make a neat garnish of bread crumbs and chopped tomatoes, or any other fine mixture, use a large chef's knife or palette knife. Place the garnishing mixture onto a clean board and scoop up some on the knife. Transfer the mixture to the salad on the horizontal knife blade. Hold the knife in position, then turn the blade vertically quite sharply to deposit the garnish in a neat line on the salad.

PASTA COOL: THE FRESHEST SALAD IDEAS

Pasta and Bean Salad

SERVES 4

8 ounces spinach-flavored fresh pasta shapes
8 ounces green beans, cut into 2-inch lengths
1 15-ounce can flageolet beans (green kidney), drained
1 red onion, halved and thinly sliced
2 tablespoons tarragon vinegar
1 teaspoon superfine sugar
salt and freshly ground black pepper
1 garlic clove, crushed
6 tablespoons olive oil
6 tablespoons croûtons

Cook the pasta in boiling salted water for 3 minutes, then drain well. Place the pasta in a bowl. Blanch the green beans in boiling salted water for 3 minutes, then drain them and add them to the pasta. Stir in the flageolet beans and onion, separating the pieces as you add them to the salad.

Shake the tarragon vinegar, sugar, seasoning and garlic in a screw-top jar. When the sugar has dissolved add the oil, put the top on the jar and shake again. Pour this dressing over the salad and toss well. Cover and leave until cold.

Just before serving, toss the salad well and mix in the croûtons. Do not leave the salad to stand after the croûtons are added or they will lose their crunch.

Spaghetti and Salami Salad

SERVES 4

12 ounces fresh spaghetti

4 tablespoons pine nuts

6 ounces salami, cut in strips

1/2 cup sliced black olives

1 15-ounce can artichoke hearts, drained

2 tablespoons cider vinegar

salt and freshly ground black pepper

1/2 teaspoon superfine sugar

6 tablespoons olive oil

4 tablespoons chopped parsley

Cut the spaghetti into 2-inch lengths, then cook it in boiling salted water for 3 minutes. Drain the pasta well in a fine strainer before tipping it into a bowl; leave to cool.

Roast the pine nuts in a small, dry, heavy-bottomed saucepan until they are lightly browned, then tip them over the pasta. Add the salami, olives and artichoke hearts. Mix the cider vinegar, seasoning and superfine sugar in a screw-top jar. Shake well until the sugar dissolves, then add the olive oil and shake again.

Pour the dressing over the salad and mix well. Toss the parsley in after the dressing, immediately before serving the salad.

93

Frankfurter Salad

SERVES 4

8 ounces fresh pasta shapes or small pasta squares
(page 14)

¹/₂ small onion, chopped

8 ounces white cabbage, shredded

2 carrots, coarsely grated

²/₃ cup mayonnaise

8 frankfurters, sliced

salt and freshly ground black pepper

4 tablespoons chopped roasted peanuts

Cook the pasta in boiling salted water for 3 minutes, then drain it and allow to cool. Mix the onion, cabbage, carrots and mayonnaise. Toss the pasta and frankfurters with the cabbage mixture and seasoning. Divide between four serving bowls. Sprinkle with peanuts and serve at once, offering plenty of warmed crusty bread with the salad.

Tagliatelle Nests

These make a good first course or light lunch.

SERVES 4

12 ounces fresh tagliatelle verdi
2 tomatoes, peeled, seeded and diced (see Cook's Tip, page 26)
2 tablespoons walnut oil
3 tablespoons sunflower oil
juice of 1 lime
salt and freshly ground black pepper
1 tablespoon chopped mint
8 ounces rindless bacon
4 ounces shelled fresh peas
4 small zucchini
4 tablespoons sour cream or fromage frais
mint sprigs, to garnish (optional)

Cook the tagliatelle in boiling salted water for 3 minutes, then drain well and turn into a bowl. Add the tomatoes, both types of oil, the lime juice, some seasoning and the mint. Toss well, cover and leave to cool.

Broil the bacon slices until they are crisp, turning once. Drain them on paper towels and leave to cool. Cook the peas in boiling water for 15 minutes, then drain and set aside. Trim the zucchini, peel them very thinly so that they are a bright green outside, then halve them lengthways. Slice the zucchini thinly and mix them with the peas.

Divide the tagliatelle and its dressing between four plates, swirling it into nests. Top the nests with the zucchini and pea mixture. Crush the crisply broiled bacon and sprinkle it over the zucchini and pea mixture, then top with a little sour cream or fromage frais. Mint sprigs may be added as a garnish, if liked.

Herbed Tomato and Pasta Salad

Served with crusty bread, this makes a splendid starter or light lunch. It does, of course, rely on fresh basil for success.

SERVES 4

8 ounces fresh pasta shapes

1 pound ripe tomatoes, peeled, seeded and quartered (see Cook's Tip, page 26)

6 scallions, chopped

1 garlic clove, crushed

salt and freshly ground black pepper

4–6 tablespoons olive oil

6 basil sprigs

Cook the pasta in boiling salted water for 3 minutes, drain and set aside to cool. Mix the tomatoes with the scallions. Add the garlic, seasoning and olive oil, and mix well. Cover and set aside to marinate for 1 hour.

Toss the tomato mixture into the pasta. Use scissors to shred the basil, with the soft stalk ends, over the pasta. Mix well and serve at once.

BELOW
Fresh ingredients on display at an Italian delicatessan.

97

Pasta and Baked Bell Pepper Salad

Skinning bell peppers is a boring task but the transformation in flavor is worth the effort. You can use any combination of bell peppers as regards color. This is another salad that makes a good first course; it is also an ideal accompaniment for barbecued meat or poultry. Instead of shop-bought pasta shapes, you can use your own small pasta squares (page 14).

SERVES 4

8 ounces fresh pasta shapes

2 red bell peppers

1 green bell pepper

1 yellow bell pepper

4 tablespoons olive oil

2 tablespoons chopped parsley

1 tablespoon lemon juice

salt and freshly ground black pepper

1 2-ounce can anchovy fillets, drained and chopped

2 eggs, hard-cooked and chopped

Cook the pasta in boiling salted water for 3 minutes, drain well, then transfer it to a shallow serving bowl.

Broil the bell peppers until they are scorched all over. This is fairly time-consuming as you have to stand and turn them to make sure that all the skin is blistered. After the skin has lifted away from the pepper flesh it can be peeled off easily and any remains should be rubbed off under cold running water.

Dry the bell peppers on paper towels, halve them and cut out all their seeds and core. Slice the bell peppers across into thin strips and scatter them over the pasta. Mix the olive oil, parsley and lemon juice with seasoning to taste. Stir in the anchovies, then use a spoon to trickle this dressing evenly over the bell peppers and pasta. Sprinkle the chopped hard-cooked egg over and serve.

Mixed Pasta Salad

A good one for all those parties and picnics!

SERVES 4

8 ounces pasta shapes

4 ounces frozen corn

4 ounces frozen peas

1 carrot, diced

4 celery stalks, diced

1 green bell pepper, seeded and diced

6 scallions, chopped

2 tablespoons chopped parsley

1 cup mayonnaise

3 tablespoons light cream

8 ounces garlic sausage, roughly chopped

salt and freshly ground black pepper

Cook the pasta in boiling salted water for 3 minutes, drain well, then place the pasta in a bowl. Place the corn, peas and carrot in a saucepan and add water to cover. Bring to a boil, add the celery and bring back to a boil, then cook for 5 minutes. Drain the vegetables and add them to the pasta. Allow to cool.

Mix in the green bell pepper, scallions and parsley. Thin the mayonnaise with the cream, then toss this dressing into the salad. Lastly, lightly mix in the garlic sausage and taste for seasoning.

CHAPTER SEVEN

PASTA INTERNATIONAL
Doughs from Around the World

This is a mere sample of the ways in which pasta-like doughs are used all over the world, in kitchens as diverse as those in China or Poland. The chapter includes a

few recipes for Chinese-style dim sum, some using the fine won ton dough from the opening chapter, and a selection of recipes for Chinese egg noodles. Eastern European pasta doughs are represented by a couple of different examples of dishes that highlight the way in which Italian culinary traditions have spread to other countries.

Most Oriental supermarkets sell fresh egg noodles and some may have fresh rice sticks, the pale, almost translucent, white pasta dough which may be cut finely, like spaghetti, or into wide ribbon noodles. Won ton wrappers are also sold ready rolled and cut into neat squares. All these pasta

types freeze well raw, and noodles can be cooked from frozen.

So if you thought fresh pasta was limited to the shapes and colors created from the same simple flour and egg dough at the beginning of the book, then read on . . . or eat on!

Won Ton Soup

SERVES 4

8 ounces ground pork
4 scallions, finely chopped
2 button mushrooms, finely chopped
2 tablespoons soy sauce
1 teaspoon sesame oil
½ quantity won ton dough (page 15)
1 egg, beaten
1 tablespoon oil
1 boneless chicken breast, skinned and diced
2 leeks, sliced
3¾ cups good chicken stock
4 tablespoons dry sherry
salt and freshly ground black pepper

Mix the pork, scallions, mushrooms, soy sauce and sesame oil. Roll out the dough into a 15-inch square, dusting the surface with cornstarch as necessary. The dough should be very thin. Cut the dough into 3-inch strips, then across into squares. Cover the dough with plastic wrap.

To fill the won tons, take a square of dough and roll it again so that it is paper-thin. Shape a little meat into a ball and place it in the middle of the dough square. Brush the meat with egg, then fold the dough around it and pinch it together to seal in the meat. Leave the corners of the dough hanging free. Fill all the won tons in the same way and place them on a platter or board dusted with cornstarch.

For the soup, heat the oil in a saucepan. Add the chicken and leeks, and cook, stirring often, for 20 minutes, until the leek is softened and the chicken is just cooked. Pour in the stock and bring to a boil. Cover and simmer for 20 minutes. Stir in the sherry and seasoning to taste. Add the won tons to the soup, bring back to a boil and reduce the heat slightly so that it does not boil fiercely. Cook for 5 minutes. Test a won ton to make sure the filling is cooked, then ladle the soup and won tons into bowls. Serve at once.

Crispy Won Tons

These won tons are made in the same way as the ones which are cooked in soup; however, they are deep-fried until crisp and served with a sweet and sour sauce. Offer them as a first course for a Chinese meal or serve them with plain boiled rice and a dish of stir-fried vegetables to make a delicious main course.

SERVES 4

won tons as for Won Ton Soup (page 101)

oil for deep frying

For the sauce

2 tablespoons oil

1 teaspoon sesame oil

1 onion, halved and thinly sliced

1 green bell pepper, halved, seeded and thinly sliced

1 carrot, cut into fine 1-inch strips

4 tablespoons tomato ketchup

4 tablespoons soy sauce

1 tablespoon superfine sugar

2 tablespoons cider vinegar

⅔ cup dry sherry

1 teaspoon cornstarch

2 canned pineapple rings, cut in small pieces

Make the won tons as for the soup. Set them aside until the sauce is ready. Heat the oil and sesame oil in a saucepan. Add the onion, green bell pepper and carrot and cook for 5 minutes. Stir in the tomato ketchup, soy sauce, sugar, cider vinegar and sherry. Bring to a boil, reduce the heat and simmer for 3 minutes. Meanwhile, blend the cornstarch with 2 tablespoons cold water, then stir it into the sauce and bring to a boil, stirring all the time. Simmer for 2 minutes, then add the pineapple and set aside over low heat.

Heat the oil for deep frying to 375°F. Deep-fry the won tons a few at a time, until they are crisp and golden. Drain them on paper towels. Place the won tons on a large flat dish or platter and spoon the sauce over them. Serve and eat at once.

LEFT
Boats on the Li River in southern China.

Chicken Won Tons with Vegetables

These are thicker than authentic won tons. This makes them easier to handle and quicker to fill – and they taste terrific! The dim sum and vegetables make an ample complete meal; if they are served with a selection of other Chinese-style dishes, then they will yield far more portions.

MAKES ABOUT 50 – SERVES 4

4 boneless chicken breasts, skinned

¹/₄ teaspoon five-spice powder

8 scallions, chopped

1 teaspoon sesame oil

5 tablespoons soy sauce

1 garlic clove, crushed

1 quantity won ton dough (page 15)

1 egg, beaten

3 tablespoons oil

2 celery stalks, cut into fine 1-inch strips

1 red bell pepper, quartered, seeded and cut in thin strips

¹/₂ medium head Chinese leaves, shredded

3 tablespoons dry sherry

Cut the chicken into 50 small pieces. Place them in a basin and add the five-spice powder, 2 table-spoons of the scallions, sesame oil, 2 tablespoons of the soy sauce and the garlic. Mix well, cover and leave to marinate for 30 minutes.

Cut the won ton dough in half. Roll out one portion into a 15-inch square. Cut the dough into 5 × 3-inch strips, then across into squares. Brush a square of dough with beaten egg. Place a piece of chicken in the middle of it, then fold the dough around the chicken and pinch it together well. Continue filling the squares, placing them on a platter dusted with cornstarch as they are ready. Roll out the second portion of dough and make a further 25 won tons.

Grease a large covered dish with oil and set it to warm. Bring a large saucepan of water to a boil, then cook the won tons in batches, allowing 5 min-utes after the water has come back to a boil. Drain, transfer to the dish and keep hot.

Stir-fry the vegetables while the won tons are cooking. Heat the oil in a large skillet. Add the celery and bell pepper, and cook, stirring, for 5 minutes. Add the remaining scallions and cook for a further 2 minutes. Then add the Chinese leaves and cook for 3–5 minutes. Pour in the remaining soy sauce and sherry, and stir for 1 minute. Arrange the vegetables and won tons together on a platter and serve at once.

Rice Sticks with Vegetables

Egg noodles may be used instead of the rice sticks. Serve this as a light lunch dish or offer it with a simple main course, such as crisp roast duck or deep-fried pork in batter.

SERVES 4

8 ounces whole baby corn
2 tablespoons oil
1 red bell pepper, seeded, quartered lengthways and thinly sliced
6 scallions, shredded diagonally
8 ounce Chinese leaves, shredded
6 ounces bean sprouts
4 tablespoons soy sauce
2 tablespoons dry sherry
12 ounces ribbon rice sticks
4 tablespoons cashew nuts, roasted
2 tablespoons sesame seeds, roasted

Blanch the baby corn in boiling water for 2 minutes, then drain. Have a large pan of boiling water ready

for cooking the rice sticks. Heat the oil in a wok or large saucepan. Add the bell pepper and scallions, and stir-fry for 3 minutes. Add the Chinese leaves and cook for 2 minutes before stirring in the bean sprouts. Pour in the soy sauce and sherry at the same time.

Add the rice sticks to the boiling water. Bring back to a boil and cook for 1 minute, then drain at once. By the time the rice sticks are ready, all the vegetables will be cooked. Place the rice sticks in a serving dish or platter. Top with the vegetables and sprinkle with the cashew nuts and sesame seeds. Serve at once.

Shrimp and Pork Dim Sum

MAKES 25

8 ounces peeled cooked shrimp, finely chopped

4 ounces ground pork

2 scallions, finely chopped

1 teaspoon sesame oil

1 garlic clove, crushed

2 teaspoons soy sauce

½ quantity won ton dough (page 15)

1 egg, beaten

soy sauce, to serve

The shrimp may be finely chopped in the food processor or blender. Mix them with the pork, scallions, sesame oil, garlic and soy sauce. Pound the mixture well so that all the ingredients bind together. Wet your hands and shape the mixture into 25 small balls.

Roll out the won ton dough into a 12.5-inch square. Dust the surface with cornstarch as necessary to prevent the dough from sticking. Cut the dough into 5 × 2½-inch strips, then cut them across into squares. Brush a square of dough with a little beaten egg. Hold the dough on the palm of your hand and place a shrimp ball on it. Flatten the shrimp ball slightly and bring the dough up and around it, leaving the top of the mixture uncovered. Brush the dough with a little extra egg, if necessary, so that the folds cling to the side of the mixture. Shape the remaining dim sum in the same way – they should have flattened bases and the dough should be wrinkled around their sides.

Place the dim sum on a greased shallow dish which will fit in a steamer, then steam them over rapidly boiling water for 15 minutes, or until the shrimp mixture is cooked. While the dim sum are cooking, prepare small dishes of soy sauce. Serve the dim sum freshly cooked: they may be dipped into the soy sauce before eating.

Mushroom Dim Sum

These are an excellent vegetarian alternative to the usual dim sum filled with pork or shrimp.

MAKES ABOUT 50 – SERVES 4

4 large Chinese dried mushrooms

4 Chinese leaves

¹/₂ × 7-ounce can water chestnuts, drained and chopped

4 scallions, chopped

1 cup finely chopped button mushrooms

1 garlic clove, crushed

2 tablespoons cornstarch

salt

1 egg, beaten

1 quantity won ton dough (page 15)

For the sauce

1 tablespoon oil

1 teaspoon sesame oil

2 scallions, chopped

1 tablespoon peeled and finely shredded fresh ginger root

1 celery stalk, cut into fine 1-inch strips

1 carrot, cut into fine 1-inch strips

sherry (see method)

2 teaspoons cornflour

2 tablespoons soy sauce

Place the dried mushrooms in a mug or very small bowl. Add just enough boiling water to cover them, then put a small saucer over them and weight it down to keep the mushrooms submerged. Leave to stand for 20 minutes. Blanch the Chinese leaves in boiling water for 30 seconds, so they are just limp. Drain and squeeze all the water from them, then chop them finely.

Drain the mushrooms, reserving the soaking liquid in a measuring cup and squeezing the water from the mushrooms. Discard any woody stalks, then chop the mushroom caps and mix them with the Chinese leaves. Add the water chestnuts, scallions, button mushrooms and garlic. Stir in the cornstarch and salt to taste. Add a little beaten egg to bind the mixture, so that it clumps easily.

Prepare a large platter for the dim sum and dust it with cornstarch. Cut the won ton dough in half. Roll out one portion into a 15-inch square, keeping the surface lightly dusted with cornstarch. Cut the dough into 5 × 3-inch strips, then across into squares. Brush a square of dough with beaten egg, then place a little of the mushroom mixture on it. Gather the dough up around the filling to make a small bundle. Press the dough together at the top to seal in the filling. Fill all the squares of dough in the same way, then roll out the second portion and repeat the process. Place the dim sum on the floured platter and cover loosely with plastic wrap while you fill the remainder.

For the sauce, heat the oil and sesame oil together in a small saucepan. Add the scallions, ginger root, celery and carrot. Stir-fry for 2 minutes. Measure the soaking liquid from the mushrooms and add enough sherry to make it up to 1¼ cups. Blend the cornstarch to a smooth, thin paste with a little of the liquid, then stir in the rest of the liquid. Pour this into the pan, add the soy sauce and bring to a boil, stirring. Reduce the heat and taste for seasoning. Leave to simmer very gently.

Bring a large saucepan of salted water to a boil. Add the dim sum, bring back to a boil and cook for 5 minutes. Do not boil the water rapidly. Drain well and place in a warmed serving dish. Ladle the sauce over the dim sum and serve.

COOK'S TIP

The dim sum cook very well by steaming but this does require a lot of steamer space. Several layers of bamboo steamer, placed on a wok, are ideal and the dim sum should be placed in greased shallow dishes or on plates. If the plates are not greased the dim sum will stick.

Glossy Dumplings

Traditionally, dumplings of this type are served with a selection of other dim sum for a light lunch or mid-afternoon snack. Serve China or Jasmine tea with the dim sum.

MAKES 24

2 Chinese dried mushrooms
6 ounces lean ground pork
1 tablespoon finely chopped fresh ginger root
1 garlic clove, crushed
1 teaspoon sesame oil
2 tablespoons finely chopped water chestnuts or celery stalks
2 scallions, finely chopped
2 tablespoons soy sauce
pinch of five-spice powder
scallion curls, to garnish

For the dough

1 cup hard flour
2 tablespoons leaf lard or white vegetable shortening

To serve

1 garlic clove, finely chopped
1 teaspoon finely chopped fresh ginger root
1 tablespoon finely chopped scallion
1 tablespoon dry sherry
about 1 cup soy sauce

Place the dried mushrooms in a cup. Add just enough boiling water to cover them, then put a small saucer over them and weight it down to keep the mushrooms submerged. Leave to stand for 20 minutes. Mix the pork, ginger root, garlic, sesame oil, water chestnuts or celery, scallions, soy sauce and five-spice powder. Drain the mushrooms, discard any woody stalks, then chop the caps finely. Add them to the pork and mix the ingredients.

To make the dough, place the flour in a basin. Measure 2 tablespoons boiling water and stir in the lard. When the lard has melted, pour the mixture into the flour and stir well to form a soft dough. Sprinkle a little cornstarch onto the work surface and knead the dough lightly, then roll it into a sausage and mark it into 24 pieces. Cut off a piece of dough to shape, then loosely cover the rest of the roll with plastic wrap.

Knead the dough briefly into a smooth ball, then flatten it into a circle measuring about 2–2½ inches across. Place a little of the meat mixture in the middle, then fold the dough over it to make a tiny dumpling in the shape of a turnover. Pinch and flute the edges to seal in the filling. Grease a shallow dish or plate and place the dumpling on it. Flatten and fill the remaining dough in the same way. Steam the dumplings over boiling water for 15 minutes, until very glossy and cooked through. Test one dumpling to make sure the filling is cooked.

While the dumplings are cooking, prepare the dipping sauces: place the garlic, ginger root, scallion and sherry in four separate dishes and top up with the soy sauce. Serve the dim sum freshly cooked, garnished with scallion curls.

COOK'S TIP

To make scallion curls, trim the roots and some of the green of scallions. Cut the green part and some of the white onion into fine shreds, leaving them all attached at the root end. Place in a bowl of iced water and leave for at least 30 minutes while the shredded scallion curls. Drain well just before using.

Crispy Chicken Chow Mein

Chow mein is a Chinese dish consisting of egg noodles mixed with other ingredients. I love this combination of textures which results from frying the noodles before topping them with sauce.

SERVES 4

4 Chinese dried mushrooms

3 boneless chicken breasts, skinned

2 tablespoons cornstarch

salt

12 ounces Chinese egg noodles

4 tablespoons oil

1 tablespoon sesame oil

1 ounce fresh ginger root, peeled and cut into short thin strips

4 celery stalks, cut into thin, 1-inch strips

1 bunch of scallions, shredded diagonally

4 tablespoons soy sauce

2/3 cup chicken stock

4 tablespoons dry sherry

Place the dried mushrooms in a mug or small bowl. Add just enough boiling water to cover them, then put a small saucer over them and weight it down to keep the mushrooms submerged. Leave to stand for 20 minutes. Drain the mushrooms, reserving the liquid, then discard any woody stems and slice the caps.

Cut the chicken into thin slices, then into fine strips. Place in a bowl or plastic bag and coat with the cornstarch, adding a little salt. Cook the noodles in a large pan of boiling salted water for 3 minutes. Drain well, then place the noodles in a large skillet and lightly pat them into a flat cake; set aside.

Heat half the oil and the sesame oil in a wok or large saucepan. Add the chicken and stir-fry until the strips are lightly browned. Add the ginger root, celery, scallions and mushrooms, and cook for a further 3 minutes. Stir in the mushrooms and add the reserved soaking liquid from the dried mush-rooms. Pour in the soy sauce and stock and bring to a boil, stirring all the time. Leave to simmer while you cook the noodles.

Slide the noodles from the skillet onto a plate. Heat the remaining oil in the skillet, then slide the noodles into it. Cook until crisp and golden under-neath. Use a large fish slice to turn the cake of noodles over. Alternatively, slide the noodle cake out onto a plate, then invert it back into the skillet. Cook the second side until crisp and golden.

Slide the noodles out onto a large platter, then pour the chicken mixture over the top. Serve at once. Diners break off portions of noodles with chopsticks or a spoon and fork, taking some of the chicken mixture with the portion. The noodles soon soften in the sauce, so they must be eaten promptly.

Pork Chow Mein

Here is another way of presenting chow mein. This time, I have used Chinese five-spice powder which, even in small quantities, gives a very strong flavor.

SERVES 4

1 pound lean boneless pork, cut into very thin 2-inch squares
2 teaspoons sesame oil
1 garlic clove
2 tablespoons soy sauce
6 tablespoons dry sherry
pinch of five-spice powder
2 tablespoons cornstarch
12 ounces fresh Chinese egg noodles
2 tablespoons oil
1 onion, halved and thinly sliced
1 green bell pepper, seeded, quartered lengthways and thinly sliced
1 7-ounce can bamboo shoots, drained and sliced
2/3 cup chicken stock

Place the pork in a bowl. Add the oil, garlic, soy sauce and 2 tablespoons of the sherry. Mix in the five-spice, cover and leave to marinate for 2 hours.

Remove the pork from the marinade and reserve the liquid. Place the meat in a plastic bag, add the cornstarch and shake the bag, holding it closed, to coat the meat evenly. Cook the noodles in boiling salted water for 3 minutes, then drain them, rinse under cold water and set aside.

Heat the oil in a wok or large skillet. Add the pork and stir-fry over fairly high heat until the pieces are evenly and lightly browned. Stir in the onion and bell pepper and continue to stir-fry for 5 minutes, until the pork is well cooked and the vegetables are softened very slightly. Stir in the bamboo shoots.

Mix the remaining sherry and stock into the reserved marinade, then pour this over the meat mixture. Bring to a boil, stirring, then add the noodles to the pan and mix well until heated through. Serve at once.

Semolina Cheese Gnocchi

Gnocchi, small Italian dumplings, are usually grouped as close relatives of pasta. There are various ways of making gnocchi and using semolina is one common method.

SERVES 4

3³/₄ cups milk
1 bay leaf
1 mace blade
1¹/₄ cups semolina
1 cup freshly grated Parmesan cheese
salt and freshly ground black pepper
2 eggs
¹/₂ stick (¹/₄ cup) lightly salted butter
shredded basil or chopped parsley, to serve

Pour the milk into a large pan and add the bay leaf and mace. Bring the milk slowly to a boil, then cover and remove from the heat. Allow the bay and mace to infuse for 45–60 minutes. Bring the milk back to just below boiling point, remove the bay and mace, then stir in the semolina. Cook, stirring all the time, until the mixture boils and thickens. It will become very stiff, so you have to work quite hard at stirring. This takes about 12–15 minutes.

Off the heat, beat in the Parmesan cheese and seasoning. Allow the mixture to cool slightly before beating in the eggs. Grease a baking sheet (a roasting pan will do) and spread the gnocchi mixture out so that it is about ¹/₂ inch thick. Cover, leave until completely cold, then chill for at least a couple of hours.

Set the oven at 400°F. Use a little of the butter to grease an ovenproof dish. Cut the gnocchi into squares and arrange them in the dish. Melt the remaining butter and trickle it over the gnocchi, then bake for 20 minutes, until golden-brown and crisp on top. Sprinkle with basil or parsley and serve at once.

Potato Gnocchi

These may be served with Meat Ragout (page 47), Good Tomato Sauce (page 56), Pesto (page 57) or Cheese Sauce (page 58). If you are looking for a simple, satisfying supper, then simply toss them with butter, freshly ground black pepper and lots of grated cheese – Parmesan or another type of your choice.

SERVES 4

1 pound potatoes
¼ stick (2 tablespoons) butter
1½ cups hard flour
1 teaspoon salt
1 egg
a little freshly grated nutmeg

Boil the potatoes in their skins until tender, about 20–30 minutes, depending on size. Drain and peel the potatoes under cold running water. Then mash them and press the mashed potato through a fine strainer into a bowl.

Add the butter to the potato and mix well. Mix in the flour and salt, then add the egg and a little nutmeg. Mix the ingredients with a spoon at first, then use your hand to bring them together into a dough. Knead lightly until smooth.

Bring a large pan of salted water to a boil. Shape a lump of the dough into a thick sausage, then cut off small pieces, about 1 inch long, and indent each piece, either with your finger or with a fork. Drop the gnocchi into the boiling water, bring back to a boil and cook for 4–5 minutes. The water must not boil too rapidly and the cooked gnocchi should be firm and tender – do not overcook them or they will become soggy and watery. Use a slotted spoon to remove the gnocchi from the pan if you are cooking them in batches. Drain well and serve at once with melted butter, pepper and freshly grated Parmesan.

Kopytka with Kabanos

Kopytka is the Polish equivalent of potato gnocchi: exact proportions of flour to potato and egg may vary slightly but the result is unmistakably similar. Here's an idea that does not pretend to be authentic to Polish cooking but does taste good. If you cannot find kabanos, use frankfurters as an alternative.

SERVES 4

1 quantity Potato Gnocchi (page 113)
2 tablespoons olive oil
2 onions, halved and thinly sliced
1 garlic clove, crushed
1 tablespoon caraway seeds
4 kabanos (about 8 ounces), sliced
1 pound sauerkraut, drained and shredded
salt and freshly ground black pepper
⅔ cup sour cream
paprika

Make and shape the gnocchi. Heat the oil in a large frying pan. Add the onions, garlic and caraway and cook for 20 minutes, until the onions are softened. Add the kabanos and sauerkraut, then cook, stirring often, for another 20 minutes.

Meanwhile, cook the gnocchi following the recipe instructions. Add the gnocchi to the kabanos and sauerkraut. Mix well and serve at once. Top each portion with sour cream and sprinkle with paprika.

Mushroom Uska

These little examples of Polish cooking are the same shape as tortellini. I have included the traditional Polish filling of dried mushrooms as it makes the most delicious pasta. For authenticity, the uska should be served in crystal clear beetroot soup; however, they are excellent tossed with butter and pepper, sour cream or a tomato sauce.

SERVES 4

1 cup hard flour
salt and freshly ground black pepper
1 egg
2 dried mushrooms (Polish or Italian)
½ cup fresh white bread crumbs
¼ stick (2 tablespoons) butter
1 small onion, finely chopped

Place the flour in a bowl with ½ teaspoon salt. Make a well in the middle, then add the egg and 1 tablespoon water. Mix to form a firm dough, using a spoon at first, then knead it by hand until smooth. Cover the dough in plastic wrap.

Simmer the mushrooms in water to cover for 5 minutes, then drain. Boil the cooking liquor until it is reduced to 2 tablespoons and set it aside. Chop the mushrooms and mix them with the bread crumbs. Melt the butter in a small saucepan, add the onion and cook, stirring, for 5 minutes. Mix the cooked onion with the mushroom mixture, the reserved liquor and seasoning to taste.

On a lightly floured surface, roll out the dough into a 12½-inch square. Cut it horizontally into 7 strips, then cut vertically to divide each strip into 7 squares. Place a little filling on each square and brush the edges of the dough with beaten egg. Fold the squares of dough in half to make triangular dumplings, sealing the edges carefully to enclose the filling. Wrap the long side of each triangle around the tip of your finger and pinch their corners together.

Bring a large saucepan of salted water to a boil. Add the uska and bring the water back to a boil. Cook for 3 minutes. Drain and serve at once.

Kopytka with Kabanos.

CHAPTER EIGHT

PASTA FOR DESSERT
Sweet Dishes to Delight

Finally, a few thoughts on sweet pasta. Depending on your culinary traditions, you will find this chapter an unexpected pleasure or simply a mere sample of the recipes that may be created.

Fruit dumplings, dusted with confectioners' sugar and served with sour cream, are classic examples of the treats from Eastern Europe where they are eaten as a light meal in their own right. From Italy come fruit compotes  *and sauces to serve with pasta. Then there are the contemporary creations, such as flavored doughs.*

If you plan to serve a substantial dessert, make the main course a light one — or simply indulge in a mid-afternoon meal instead of lunch one day and make a selection of sweet filled pasta!

Hidden Plums

Fruit dumplings of this type, encased in a dough made of potato and boiled as for ravioli, are typical of Eastern European cooking. Keep the main course simple and light when serving these for dessert as they are quite filling.

SERVES 4

1 pound potatoes
½ cup hard plain flour
1 egg
12 firm plums
3 ounces white almond paste
½ stick (¼ cup) unsalted butter
confectioners' sugar for dredging
1¼ cups sour cream

BELOW
Villagers from Dzianisz, Poland, returning from church.

Boil the potatoes in their skins for 20 minutes, or until tender. Drain and peel them, then press them through a fine strainer. Mix in the flour. Make sure the mixture is not too hot for the egg before mixing it in to make a dough. Knead the dough together, then cut it into 12 equal portions. Keep the dough covered when you are not working with it.

Slit the plums down one side and remove their pits. (If the pits do not come out easily you will have to halve the plums, but this is less successful.) Divide the almond paste into 12 small pieces and place a little in the middle of each plum. Flatten a portion of dough, place a plum on it, then knead it around the fruit to enclose it completely. Pinch the dough to seal it thoroughly.

Bring a large saucepan of water to a boil. Melt the unsalted butter and set it aside over very low heat to keep hot without cooking. Add the plums and cook for 3–5 minutes, drain them well, then spoon them into a heated serving dish. Pour the butter over and dredge the plums thickly with confectioners' sugar. Serve immediately, offering sour cream with the hidden plums.

THE FRESH PASTA COOKBOOK

Rum and Raisin Shapes

SERVES 6

½ cup chopped raisins

1½ tablespoons finely chopped candied peel

¾ cup ground almonds

2 tablespoons confectioners' sugar

8 tablespoons rum

⅔ quantity pasta dough (page 14)

1 egg, beaten

½ cup crab apple jelly

4 tablespoons unsweetened apple juice

2 tablespoons finely chopped candied orange peel, to decorate

Greek-style yogurt or cream, to serve

Mix the raisins, candied peel, ground almonds and confectioners' sugar. Stir in enough of the rum to bind the ingredients together; the rest of the rum is required for the glaze.

Roll out, cut and fill the pasta as for Spiced Apricot Rounds (page 123). When all the pasta is filled, cook in boiling water for 5 minutes and drain well. To make the glaze, gently heat the crab apple jelly with the apple juice until the jelly melts. Bring to a boil, then remove from the heat and stir in the remaining rum.

Serve the pasta coated with the apple glaze. Sprinkle with the chopped candied orange peel and offer Greek-style yogurt or cream with the pasta.

Plum and Blackberry Compote

A good sauce for serving with plain homemade pasta in the fall. Remember that dessert pasta looks more attractive if it is stamped out in pretty shapes using aspic cutters.

SERVES 6

½ cup granulated sugar
grated peel and juice of 1 orange
⅔ cup dry cider
1 cinnamon stick
2 cloves
1 pound plums, halved and pitted
1 pound blackberries

Place the sugar, orange peel and juice, cider, cinnamon and cloves in a large saucepan. Heat gently, stirring, until the sugar melts. Allow the syrup to infuse over very low heat for 15 minutes, then bring it to simmering point and add the plums.

Poach the plums gently for 3 minutes, then add the blackberries and cook for 2 minutes. (Do not overcook the fruit until it becomes soft; the cooking time for the plums varies according to their texture.) Ladle this fruit sauce over the pasta, removing the spices as you do so.

Chocolate Bows with White Chocolate Sauce

The unusual combination of the pasta texture and sweet flavor may not be to everyone's liking but chocolate fans will approve.

SERVES 4

1/3 quantity pasta dough (page 14)
2 tablespoons unsweetened cocoa powder
3 tablespoons confectioners' sugar
1 tablespoon walnut oil
1 teaspoon natural vanilla extract
8 ounces white chocolate
3 tablespoons light corn syrup
1/4 stick (2 tablespoons) unsalted butter
1/2 cup chopped walnuts

Make the pasta dough, adding the cocoa powder and confectioners' sugar to the flour before mixing in the egg and using 1 tablespoons walnut oil and the vanilla extract instead of the olive oil. Roll out the dough into a 12-inch square.

Cut the dough into 1½-inch strips, then cut them across into 1½-inch squares. Pinch the opposite corners of a square of dough together, pleating the dough in the middle of the square and pressing it firmly, to make a small bow with pointed ends. Set the bow aside on a surface dusted with confectioners' sugar. Do not cover the bows.

Before cooking the bows, prepare the white chocolate sauce. Break the chocolate into squares and place in a heatproof bowl. Add the light corn syrup and butter, then stand the bowl over a small saucepan of barely simmering water. Stir until the chocolate melts and the sauce is smooth. Turn the heat off and set the pan and bowl aside.

Cook the bows in just-boiling water for 3 minutes. Meanwhile, pour some chocolate sauce on warmed plates. Drain the bows, then arrange them on the sauce. Sprinkle with nuts and serve at once.

Chocolate Fruit Dreams

SERVES 6

*⅓ quantity plain pasta dough (page 14) or
1 quantity chocolate pasta dough
(see Chocolate Bows, page 120)*

8 ounces strawberries, sliced

6 tablespoons maple syrup

8 ounces raspberries

1¼ cups whipping cream, whipped

2–3 tablespoons toasted chopped hazelnuts

Make the pasta dough, roll it into a 12-inch square and cut it into 1-inch strips. Cut the strips at an angle to make diamond shapes (rather like cutting almond paste leaves when decorating a cake). Cook the pasta in boiling water for 3 minutes, then drain it well.

In a bowl, mix the sliced strawberries with the maple syrup. Add the drained pasta and mix lightly. Mix the raspberries with the pasta and strawberries, taking care to keep them whole. Divide the fruit and pasta between 6 dishes. Top with generous swirls of cream, then sprinkle with toasted chopped hazelnuts. Serve at once.

Spiced Apricot Rounds

SERVES 6

2 cups finely chopped ready-to-eat dried apricots
1 teaspoon ground cinnamon
2 tablespoons confectioners' sugar
grated peel and juice of 1 orange
2/3 quantity pasta dough (page 14)
1 egg, beaten
5 tablespoons clear honey
1/2 cup slivered almonds, toasted
1 teaspoon cinnamon or allspice
orange slices, to decorate
whipped cream, to serve

Mix the apricots, cinnamon or allspice, confectioners' sugar and orange peel. Cut the dough in half and roll out one portion into a 12-inch square.

Use a 2-inch round fluted cutter or a shaped cutter to stamp out pieces of dough. If you work neatly, you will get 36 shapes.

Brush a piece of dough with the beaten egg, place a little of the apricot mixture in the middle, then cover with a second piece of dough. Pinch the edges together firmly to seal in the filling. Continue until all the shapes are used, then repeat with the second portion of dough. Place the finished rounds on a plate lightly dusted with cornstarch and keep them loosely covered while you fill the other shapes.

Bring a large saucepan of water to a boil and cook the pasta in batches for 5 minutes each. Drain well. While the pasta is cooking, heat the orange juice and honey. Serve the hot pasta coated with the honey and orange juice and sprinkled with the toasted slivered almonds. Decorating individual plates with attractive pieces of sliced orange improves the appearance of the dessert. Serve with whipped cream.

Summer Fruit Sauce

Serve this sauce with pasta shapes, either bought or homemade. Instead of pouring the sauce over the pasta, ladle the sauce into dishes, then top it with pasta and sprinkle with chopped nuts and confectioners' sugar.

SERVES 4

8 ounces redcurrants
1/3 cup superfine sugar
juice of 1 orange
8 ounces strawberries, halved
8 ounces raspberries
mint sprigs, to decorate

Place the redcurrants, sugar and orange juice in a saucepan. Heat gently until the sugar dissolves, then bring to a boil. Cook gently for 1 minute, then remove from the heat.

Mix the strawberries and raspberries into the redcurrants. Add the mint sprigs, if liked, and mix lightly, then pick them out to use as a decoration when serving the sauce.

LEFT
Spiced Apricot Rounds.

GLOSSARY

Agnolotti A name sometimes used for round filled pasta (see Ravioli).

Al Dente The Italian term used to describe the texture of pasta which is perfectly cooked: tender but not soft, with a bit of bite or resistance.

Bain Marie A container of hot water in which to stand a dish during baking. The outer container of water protects the contents of the dish from fierce heat which may spoil delicate foods, such as custards or light mixtures set with egg. A bain marie may also be used on the hob.

Bamboo Shoots Oriental ingredient sold prepared in cans. Canned bamboo shoots may be packed in large, semi-circular chunks or cut into fine slices. They may be used in a wide variety of dishes, including chow mein.

Basil Fragrant, full-flavored herb with large, bright green, tender leaves. The leaves bruise easily, losing texture and some of their flavor in chopping, so they are best shredded using scissors. The soft stalk ends may also be finely snipped and used. The flavor of basil diminishes on cooking, so it is usually added late in the preparation of a dish. The flavor of dried basil does not compare well with that of the fresh herb so it is best avoided in this form. Buy growing pots or plant a large potful outside in summer months. Preserve any excess by making pesto (page 57).

Bay Leaves Evergreen shrub of laurel family. The leaves have a distinct flavor which is excellent in many savory dishes and some sweet puddings. Bay leaves also freeze well or the dried herb may be used.

Bean Sprouts Sprouted mung beans, harvested when the shoots are about 1–2 inches long and still white. They are crunchy and delicately flavored, and may be used raw or very lightly cooked in a wide range of dishes including chow mein. Mung beans may be sprouted by first soaking overnight in cold water, then draining and keeping moist in a part-covered jam jar for 2–3 days. The beans must be rinsed with water every day and kept in a warm place so that they germinate. The jar may be covered with a piece of white cotton, kept in place with an elastic band.

Bows Another name sometimes used for butterfly pasta shapes. You can make these by hand, by cutting small squares of thinly rolled pasta and pinching or twisting each one in the middle.

Cannelloni Dried cannelloni are wide tubes about 4 inches long; however, fresh cannelloni are made by cutting sheets of pasta and rolling them around the filling.

Cardamoms An aromatic, mild spice. The small pale green pods consist of a papery covering which conceals compartments filled with small black seeds. The whole pods are added to dishes and they may be chewed. They have a refreshing, zesty, lemon-ginger flavor which is used in both savory and sweet cooking.

Chick Peas Small round dried pulses, pale cream in color with indented sides. They require soaking overnight before boiling in water for about 50 minutes, or until tender; alternatively, canned chick peas have an excellent texture. Their nutty flavor is good with pasta and their high protein content is valuable in main dishes.

Chicory In American cookery this is a frilly, firm-texture lettuce-like vegetable; in British cookery, this term is used for endive.

Chilies There are many types of chilies, varying in hotness, from extremely fiery types to mild chilies. The small, wiry chilies are often very hot; canned jalapeño chilies are fairly mild. As well as heat, chilies have a distinct peppery flavor which is most apparent in the milder types. The seeds are especially hot, so cut out the core and rinse away all seeds before use. Always wash your hands after handling chilies as their juices are highly irritating, causing an excruciating, burning sensation when in contact with sensitive areas, such as eyes, or any grazed skin or cuts.

Chinese Dried Mushrooms Although several types of dried fungus are used in Chinese cooking, this term refers to dried shiitake mushrooms. The cap, which varies in size from 1 to 3 inches, is dark outside and the stalks are usually very woody. They have a slightly musty flavor which adds a rich, distinctive characteristic taste to oriental dishes. These mushrooms must be soaked for at least 15 minutes, then drained and the stalks removed before cooking. The soaking liquor is often kept and used to flavor sauces.

Chinese Egg Noodles Fine round noodles made from a rich egg dough. Available fresh from oriental supermarkets, these freeze extremely well. The noodles cook in 1–2 minutes in boiling water, slightly longer if frozen.

Chinese Leaves Tall, crinkly and closely packed vegetable, almost a cross between a cabbage and a lettuce. The pale green leaves have a wide white central "vein" which is crisp and crunchy to eat. May be shredded and used raw or lightly cooked.

Chives Herb which resembles fine round grass, this has an onion-like flavor. Snip into very short lengths using scissors instead of chopping.

Chow Mein A Chinese noodle dish. The noodles may be soft or they may be shallow-fried after cooking until partly crisped.

Cider Vinegar Vinegar prepared from an apple base, this is less harsh than malt vinegar or wine vinegar.

Cilantro Leaves Fresh herb grown from coriander seeds, this resembles flat-leafed parsley in appearance but it has a strong flavor.

Cinnamon Sweet spice using in savory and sweet cooking. Obtained from the bark of a tree, cinnamon is sold as sticks, which is the rolled bark stripped of the rough outer covering, or ground. Cinnamon is also available as rough pieces of unstripped bark. Sticks and bark are removed from dishes before eating.

Coconut Milk Made by soaking coconut flesh in boiling water, then draining and squeezing out all the liquid. Fresh or unsweetened shredded coconut may be used. However, it is easier to buy instant coconut milk in powder form. Creamed coconut, sold as blocks or cans, may also be melted or diluted in hot water to make coconut milk. Instant powder is most convenient and it has the longest shelf life before the packet is opened.

Coriander Aromatic spice with mild flavor. Small round, pale seeds about the size of peppercorns which may be crushed, or ready ground types are available.

Crimini Mushrooms See Mushrooms.

Croûtons Small cubes or shapes of fried bread, used as a garnish or to add a contrast in texture to dishes.

Cumin Small, slim, oval seeds with a distinct flavor; usually white (creamy, in fact) although black seeds are also available. Ground cumin has a strong flavor.

Curry Powder A mixture of spices, including fenugreek, coriander, cumin, cinnamon, chili powder, turmeric and cloves. Curry powder is a British invention to use instead of mixing individual spices to achieve a specific flavor in a dish, which is authentic to Indian cooking. When buying curry powder, look for a good-quality brand with a mild flavor and it is useful for pepping up Western-style dishes.

Dates, fresh These have firm flesh and a papery skin which is easily rubbed or peeled off. Halve the dates or slit them down one side to remove the long thin pits. Good with goat's cheese: slice them and toss them with crumbled goat's cheese and pasta for a delicious light meal.

Dill Feathery herb which resembles fennel in appearance but bears no relationship flavor-wise. Fresh dill has a delicate, distinctive flavor which is excellent with seafood or eggs. Dried dillweed is so inferior that it is not worth using: it has a "green" taste that somehow imparts a grass-like image to a dish. Freeze fresh dill for use in sauces; use from frozen.

Dim Sum Chinese snacks, including little dumplings made from a pasta-like dough.

Dolcelatte A creamy blue cheese of the Gorgonzola family but far milder. Delicious with pasta, either gently melted into warm cream to make a rich sauce or diced and tossed with hot, buttery pasta.

Dried Mushrooms Boletus or cep (or porcini in Italian) are available dried in slices or smaller pieces. They are soaked before use and the soaking water should be retained to flavor sauces. There are other types of dried mushroom to be found in delicatessens, some strung up whole. They have a strong flavor, so are used in small quantities.

Fettucine Ribbon noodles, also known as tagliatelle.

Five-spice Powder A Chinese spice which is extremely strong. As its name implies, the powder consists of five spices, including star anise, cloves, cinnamon, fennel and anise pepper. Use this sparingly.

Flageolet Beans Small, oval, pale green pulses. They have a delicate flavor which goes well with pasta. Buy dried and soak overnight, then boil them for about 45 minutes or use canned. Good also with lamb, mint and pasta.

Frisée Another name for chicory, the frilly lettuce.

Fromage Frais Fresh, unripened cheese which is soft and creamy. May be used instead of cream but it curdles quickly on heating, so should not be allowed to approach simmering point in a sauce. Various fat levels are available, from virtually nonfat to rich, creamy fromage frais with a high fat content.

Ginger root, fresh Knobbly root which has a beige skin. When young, the skin is thin and the flesh zesty and tender. Older, tough ginger root which is wrinkled and softened is not worth buying. The flavor is slightly lemony and slightly hot – but large quantities of fresh ginger root have to be used before a hot flavor is imparted to a dish.

Gnocchi A type of pasta made from soft dough, shaped into small pieces and boiled. Semolina or potato may be used as the base; or a dough of ricotta cheese and spinach may be shaped into gnocchi.

Jalapeño Chilies See chilies.

Lasagne Wide strips or squares of pasta.

Mace Spice which forms a net-like covering around nutmeg. It is available dried in orange-colored pieces, known as blades, or ground. Excellent with duck, game, meat and sausage meat dishes.

Marjoram Sweet herb with a distinct flavor that is typical of Mediterranean dishes. Fresh or dried may be used, the fresh herb has a mild flavor.

Mint Familiar herb which is best fresh or frozen as the dried type has a slightly inferior flavor.

Mozzarella Cheese Small round cheeses with a rubbery texture and delicious creamy, very mild flavor. They are unripened. Traditionally made from buffalo milk. Buy only Italian mozzarella as it is superior to some other types (for example, Danish mozzarella has an inferior flavor and texture). Used in salads, as a pizza topping and for baking on pasta dishes.

Mushrooms There are many types of edible mushrooms; however, the familiar fresh mushrooms also vary. Button mushrooms that are very small are ideal for cooking whole or halved. They are pale and mild in flavor. Slightly larger button mushrooms which are nominally darker in color are ideal for slicing. Field mushrooms or large open cap mushrooms are dark with large caps. They may be stuffed or broiled, or sliced for using in a dark sauce as they have a good flavor. However they will discolor a pale sauce.

Crimini mushrooms are medium in size with closed caps which are brown rather than beige in color. They have a slightly stronger flavor than regular button or closed cap mushrooms.

Specialty varieties include oyster mushrooms which are soft, pale and delicate. They are large flat, fan-shaped caps which are delicate in appearance and flavor. They should be cooked briefly, by poaching or sautéing. They are ideal in a mixed mushroom dish.

Nutmeg Hard, round nut which is grated on a small grater. The spice has a sweet, strong flavor which is valued in savory and sweet cooking. Good with cheese and in milk sauces.

Olive Oil An essential adjunct to fresh Italian pasta. Whole books have been devoted to olive oil as there is so much to say about the production and quality of the ingredient.

In brief, oils vary significantly: dark green extra virgin olive oil is taken from the first pressing of the olives. It has a rich flavor which is delicious with garlic and Parmesan cheese to dress fresh pasta. Lighter colored oil which is taken from successive pressings has less flavor.

Most supermarkets offer a range of qualities, price and color being a good indication of flavor, and superior varieties are sold in some delicatessens. It is worth buying a small bottle of rich olive oil if you like the flavor – smell the oil and you will notice the difference before you taste the sweetness in its flavor. Average quality olive oil is fine for cooking; look for a mixture of olive and sunflower oil if you find the flavor of olive oil alone rather overpowering.

Oregano Wild marjoram, a strongly flavored herb which is good with most pasta dishes. Dried may be used instead of fresh.

Paglia e Fieno Narrow spinach (verdi) and white noodles combined, the Italian name means straw and hay.

Parmesan Cheese Strong, hard cheese which should be bought in a chunk, then grated as required. Alternatively, process chunks of Parmesan in a food processor until fine, then freeze and remove small amounts as required. Fresh Parmesan has a sweet flavor which cannot be compared with the harsh odor and strong tang of dry, grated Parmesan which is sold in cartons.

Parsley Familiar herb which is available fresh all year; chop a large batch and freeze to use from frozen.

Pasta Shapes, fresh There is a limited variety of manufactured (extruded) shapes available in fresh pasta, including spirals or twists and penne as well as the usual spaghetti, noodles and paglia e fieno. Make your own unorthodox alternatives by cutting rolled pasta dough into small squares or shredding it into oblong pieces.

Penne Or quills, these are short, narrow tubes with ends cut at a slant.

Peppercorns Dried peppercorns are available as widely used black or less often white, both of which give a better flavor when used freshly ground. Dried green peppercorns are lighter and easily crushed. Red or pink peppercorns are similar in size but they are not of the same family. Pickled green peppercorns are available in brine. Fresh green peppercorns are also available occasionally, sold on their stalks: they have a strong but refreshing pepper flavor.

Pine Nuts Small oval, pale cream-colored seeds which have a nutty flavor. They are used plain, for example in pesto, or may be roasted for use in a variety of sauces or dishes.

Pistachio Oil Bright green oil from pistachio nuts, this has a strong flavor and should be used sparingly.

Ravioli Round or square shapes of stuffed pasta, depending on the region of origin.

Rice Sticks Traditional Chinese and Japanese pasta made from rice flour. They are white in color and may be transparent, widths range from wide ribbon noodles to very fine vermicelli. They cook quickly and have a very light flavor and texture. Available fresh from oriental supermarkets.

Ricotta Cheese A light soft cheese which differs from the ordinary cheeses in that it is made from the whey rather than the curds. It does not melt and run during cooking. Used in fillings for pasta and in gnocchi dough.

Rosemary Strongly flavored herb with short, dark-green spikes which sprout along woody stems. Dried is quite woody in texture. Good with pork and lamb.

Sage Herb with soft, pale green leaves and a peppery flavor. Good with pork, vegetables and cheese.

Salsa A Mexican term for a spicy fresh sauce.

Sauerkraut Salted white cabbage available in jars. Squeeze out excess brine, then hold the sauerkraut in a firm bundle and slice it to form shreds.

Spaghetti Fine round strands of pasta, fresh spaghetti is sold curled in packets.

Spirals or Twists The most common fresh pasta shapes.

Sun-dried Tomatoes Available in packages, the tomatoes are easily cut up by shredding using scissors. They impart a rich flavor to dishes. Soak them in liquid or olive oil to soften (some are packed in olive oil) or simmer in a sauce.

Tagliatelle Ribbon noodles.

Tahini A beige-colored paste made from sesame seeds.

Thyme Familiar, small-leafed herb with a strong flavor. Use fresh or dried.

Tofu Also known as bean curd, this is prepared from soya beans. It is sold in blocks, displayed in chiller cabinets. The natural curd is tasteless and it readily absorbs the flavor of other ingredients with which it is cooked. Smoked or flavored tofu is also available.

Tortellini Small stuffed pasta shapes enclosing a little filling. They are shaped by stuffing squares or rounds of pasta and sealing in a triangular shape, then pinching long ends together.

Turmeric Bright yellow spice ground from a root of the same color. It has a distinct, mild flavor.

Walnut Oil Strongly flavored oil which should be used sparingly as a flavoring rather than for frying. It can also be used to add a nutty flavor to pasta dough or added to sauces.

Water Chestnuts Small, rounded and white when prepared, canned water chestnuts have a crisp texture and a light, nutty flavor. They are used in oriental cooking, especially in stir-frying, usually sliced.

Won Tons Small Chinese dumplings made from a light pasta-like dough with a small amount of filling. These dumplings may be simmered in water or stock or deep-fried.

Yam Large root vegetable with a crisp, papery skin which is peeled off using a knife to reveal the white flesh which is slightly slimy when raw. Cut into pieces and boil in salted water for 10–20 minutes, depending on the size of the pieces, until tender. Drain; the vegetable is rather like very floury potatoes.

INDEX